THE WORLD'S BEST ROSES

Orietta Sala

THE WORLD'S
BEST
ROSES

PRENTICE HALL GARDENING

NEW YORK   LONDON   TORONTO
SYDNEY   TOKYO   SINGAPORE

PRENTICE HALL
15 Columbus Circle
New York, New York, 10023

Library of Congress Cataloging-in-Publication Data

Sala, Orietta,
    [1000 rose.   English]
    The world's best roses / Orietta Sala.
       p.   cm.
    Translation of: 1000 rose.
    Includes bibliographical references and index.
    ISBN 0-13-636259-1 (hardcover) : $45.00
    1. Roses—Varieties. 2. Roses—Pictorial works. 3. Roses.
 I. Title.
 SB411.6.S2513   1991
 635.9'33372—dc20   91-13983
                                 CIP

ISBN: 0-13-636259-1

First Prentice Hall Edition

Contents

Rosa centifolia

The Long Road
Toward the Modern Rose

Origins and Evidence

The history that leads from wild rose species to today's roses, first through spontaneous mutations and crosses, and then through hybridizations and selections undertaken in recent centuries, is long, complicated, and often confusing. No other plant can boast of having a past so venerable and full of adventure. The rose, it seems, is no longer a flower in the sense of a simple creation of nature, but rather is a sophisticated product, slowly molded over the centuries by the passionate work of man.

Science gives us proof of the existence of the rose in the Tertiary period: roses have been discovered in the Baltic basin that date back 20 million years, and fossil roses have been found in India, Oregon, and Colorado. Literature, history, art, poetry, and archaeological finds for the most ancient periods, all offer evidence of the importance of this flower, whose life, both in reality and symbolism, is closely connected with that of man.

In China, the rose has been cultivated for more than 5,000 years. In Chaldea, in the third millennium before Christ, King Sargon of Ur had it written on a tablet that he had brought back "roses, vines, and figs" from a military expedition. Even Queen Hatshesput of the 18th Dynasty of Egypt sent ships to the far-distant lands of the Punt in search of rare plants, especially roses. Roses appear on frescoes in the palace at Cnossus, in Crete. Achille's shield is adorned with roses, as described in the Iliad. Confucius possessed 600 volumes in his library on the cultivation of the rose, which Sapho·had already declared to be "the queen of flowers." At Rhodes, whose name means "rose" (from the Greek *rodon*), this flower, emblem of the city, appeared on coins.

Legends, myths, and poems have always celebrated the rose in the gentlest of tones. But the rose has need only of her name to be distinguished. Thus, the greatest praise that can be accorded her is the phrase from the American writer Gertrude Stein: "A rose is a rose is a rose is a rose."

Roses in Ancient Times

The rose's native habitat embraces the entire northern hemisphere, never extending below the Equator; the family is especially abundant in Europe, Asia Minor, Central and Eastern Asia, and North America. However, it is primarily in China and the Middle East that several species were the object of cultivations of particular interest, and became the point of departure for all future development. From Asia Minor these roses moved to the Greek world, and then to Rome and all of Europe.

Theophrastus's work represents the most reliable text for learning about the roses that were cultivated in ancient times. He refers to roses with single corollas and roses with many petals, white roses, pink roses, and fragrant roses. Herodotus speaks of a very fragrant mythical rose that grew in King Midas's gardens and that had one hundred petals. The Latin term *centifolia* obviously refers to the petals and not the leaves, though the true *centifolia* rose appeared several centuries later. Even the naturalist Pliny lists the roses of his time, and mentions the red rose of Miletus, the rose of Preneste, and the rose of Carthage. The rose of Paestum is spoken of by Virgil, who said that it flowered in winter and is the *Rosa × bifera,* that is, with two flowerings each year.

Rosa gallica

In the Greek and Roman worlds the rose was cultivated for pleasure, and we find it as the symbol for beauty, grace, perfection, and pure love, as well as for the passion of love. But here it is also a luxury object and one for refined pleasures, and thus cultivated widely in order to satisfy many needs: to produce perfumes, essences, scented water for bathing, and oils for massage; to satisfy the constant request for cut flowers, the ornament for all feasts, banquets, and triumphal rites; and even to please the whimsical appetites of the rich and powerful. The accounts of how Anthony and Cleopatra swam every day in pools filled with rose petals are well known, as are those of crazed emperors suffocating senators under a shower of roses.

For years authors, botanists, and other horticultural and historical experts have persisted in trying to identify precisely the roses of the ancients, and there is agreement on several types. Certainly present in the gardens and cultivations of the Greeks and Romans were the *Rosa gallica,* the red rose *par excellence* and perhaps the most ancient. Also found were several of her forms, including the *officinalis,* which was not only the rose of medicinal virtues, but also the sacred rose for many peoples such as the Medes and Persians. Also present in summer was the *damask,* a very elegant rose for its corollas, tapered buds, and its high, noble, and open growth. This rose probably resulted from a spontaneous cross of *Rosa gallica* and *Rosa phoenicea,* and was thus already a hybrid. The ancients knew of double forms of the *damask,* which are the *centifolia* spoken of by Theophrastus and Herodotus.

The Autumn *Damask* on the other hand—Virgil's famous *Rosa × bifera*—appears to have also descended from the *Rosa gallica,* though this time married to the *Rosa moschata.* The *Rosa moschata* may have originated in Asia Minor and the Himalayas, and was cultivated in ancient India and probably naturalized in the Mediterranean basin. In any event, *moschata* is a rose whose parentage remains shrouded in mystery.

The theories regarding the *Rosa × alba* are even more tenuous; perhaps the ancients knew of it, and certainly it was known in the Middle Ages (the white rose of England identifies itself with the *alba*). It is certain, given the chromosomal evidence, that her parents are the *Rosa canina,* the most widely diffused of Europe's wild roses, crossed with a *damask.* The *albas* are roses having a thick gray-green foliage, soft corollas, and colors limited to white and pale pink.

The *foetida* and *foetida bicolor* roses, later named "Austrian copper," are from Persia and south Asia. They did not play any particular role in ancient times, where yellow roses are never mentioned, but took on an important role later during the era of the great hybridizations. Dioscorides, however, mentions them in his medical work, also citing another rose native to Europe, the *Rosa sempervirens.*

Roses from the Middle Ages to the 18th Century

With the fall of the ancient world, and through the long, dark Middle Ages, medicinal herbs, flowers, and plants found asylum in the cloisters of monasteries and imperial gardens. The rose was among those flowers, and it remained queen in the hearts of men, in poetry, and in art.

We do not have much evidence of its cultivation in the West, though some rose gardens are mentioned. Saint Venantius Fortunatus celebrated the garden of the wife of Clotaire I at Poitiers, and Charlemagne's list of plants for his palaces begins with roses and lilies.

After the year 1000, Albert the Great mentions the *gallica* roses and even the double *alba;* Crescentius also speaks of these. The Arab doctor Avicenna confirms for us that in Syria vast expanses of land were dedicated to the cultivation of the rose. The region of Provins, near Paris, became the center of a flourishing cultivation of both *gallica officinalis,* or the Apothecary's Rose, and the double *gallica.* Also famous in this period is the speckled version, *Rosa gallica versicolor,* or 'Rosa Mundi'.

There are countless testimonies to the emblematic force acquired by the rose. Painting, architecture, sacred and profane literature; all the art man has left as a testimony to himself speaks forever of the rose. The rose is found in jewels, in paintings of Virgins and Madonnas, in ornaments and clothing, carpets and tapestries, on church facades and friezes, in missals and books of hours, in illuminations, novels, and poems. In English heraldry we find the red rose of the Lancasters and the white rose of the Yorks, the celebrated roses of the Hundred Years' War. It is in the Christian religion that the rose achieves its highest honor; it is dedicated to the cult of Mary, wherein it takes on the mantle of the Mystical Rose, without sin.

Among those whose writings lingered on roses were such authorities on plants as Dioscorides, a Greek doctor in Nero's army, whose books were disseminated in translations during the Renaissance; William Turner, called the father of English botany, who named several varieties of rose including *alba,* as the 'Incarnation Rose' (which would become 'Maiden's Blush'), and the *alba semi-plena;* and, above all, John Parkinson, in whose

Rosa chinensis "Old Blush"

works *Paradisus Terrestris* (1629) and *Theatrum Botanicum* (1640) some thirty types of roses then being cultivated were finally specified. He recognized the Preneste rose of the Romans to be a *damask* and declared that Miletus's rose and that of Provins were double *gallicas*. He speaks of other *gallicas, albas,* and *moschata;* of the *Rosa eglanteria* (that is, the *églantine* of the French) and the Brier of the English, and of the Burnet rose or Scotch rose (these were primarily the *Rosa spinosissima* or *Rosa pimpinellifolia);* he also speaks of two *centifolia* and of a rose that had already arrived from America, the *Rosa virginiana.*

There was much controversy regarding the *Rosa centifolia* and its origins. John Gerard, a pharmacist for the Stuart James I, claims to have cultivated it in his own garden, and Clusius informs us that this rose had appeared in his country, Holland, in the 16th century. Through the evidence of literature and art, *R. centifolia* slowly evolved from the end of the 16th century to the beginning of the 18th century, when it became one of the most popular roses of the time, due largely to the efforts of the Dutch breeders. At the end of the 16th century the French claimed it as their property, baptizing it the "Rose of Provence," because they cultivated it in that region, and the Dutch claimed to have obtained it through hybridization.

What is certain is that this is a much hybridized rose, with a complicated chromosome complement that relates it to the *canina,* the *gallica,* and the *alba,* as well as to the *moschata,* the *damask,* the *phoenicea.* It is a sterile rose, since its stamens are transformed to form the dense central rosette.

During the 17th century, the Dutch developed an additional two hundred varieties of *centifolia,* whose sumptuous corollas languidly bend over onto the stem. Many other cultivars bear French names, such as the famous 'Fantin Latour', which the painter portrayed in many of his works, just as the 'Rose des Peintres' appears in many Flemish paintings.

There are dwarf *centifolia,* with small, exquisite diamond-shaped flowers: 'Rose des Meaux' and 'Pompon de Bourgogne'. Of particular interest is a *centifolia* discovered accidentally in an English garden around 1770, 'Unique Blanche', which compares favorably with many modern hybrids.

The history of the *centifolia* would be incomplete if we did not mention one of their spontaneous mutations, the *Rosa centifolia muscosa.* Turner, among other authors, speaks of this rose, leaving us with uncertainty regarding its precise identification. The *muscosa* is a rose that presents a curious characteristic (also shared by some damasks) of having its stems and calyxes covered by a thick down, full of essence glands that give off a musky scent—hence the name. The first and oldest *muscosa* are the red 'Common Moss', the 'White Moss', and a streaked variety. In the 19th century, several hybridizers occupied themselves with the *muscosa,* creating numerous varieties that fashion would make quite popular.

Chinese Roses

The roses originating in Eastern countries certainly did not come to life only when they were introduced to Europe by travelers and by the intense maritime traffic that connected the two continents during the 19th century. Chinese literature is rich in references to the rose and her species, references perhaps thousands of years old.

However, it was only at the end of the 18th century that the Asian roses became available to the West, leading the rose toward her dazzling future. Mainly responsible for this change was the *Rosa chinensis,* with its various forms. The species called 'Old Blush' was already depicted in a herbarium in 1733, and cultivated a bit later in both the Chelsea Physic Gardens and at Kew; and the *Rosa gigantea* from Burma was enormous in size and thrived in hot weather. It is not the *chinensis* and *gigantea* themselves, but four hybrids from these two species, that marked the beginning of the high season for the new roses. In texts these are mentioned as "stud roses," and in addition to being identified by the name of the gentlemen who welcomed them to London, their names also include a color reference.

The first such hybrid, introduced in 1792, is the 'Crimson China' by Slater, crimson and always in bloom (and from which the Portland Rose would derive). The second, arriving in London in 1793, is the 'Pink China' by Parson. Specimens of the 'Pink China' were also brought to the French colonies where they contributed to the birth of the Bourbon Roses, and to America where they were used to create the Noisette Roses. The third of these hybrids, the tea-scented 'Blush China' by Hume, arrived in 1810, but is no longer cultivated today. Finally, in 1824, Parks's gold-colored (and also tea-scented) 'Yellow China' arrived. These latter two Chinese roses would lead to the creation of the Tea Rose in Europe, and thus to the subsequent Hybrid Teas.

The first Western Tea Roses appeared around 1830, and the last during the first decade of the 20th century. They are characteristically very fragrant, refined, and aristocratic, both for their natural elegance and the fact that they are cultivated in the gardens, hothouses,

Rosa banksiae alba

and villas of noble families on the Riviera. These are pale and fragile roses, many of whose names have been forgotten. Some, though, are remembered, among them 'Safrano', 'Niphetos', and 'Duchesse de Brabant'. During this century the glory of their own cousins, the Portlands, Noisettes, and Bourbons (also daughters of the same Chinese roses), has dimmed. With the advent of the Hybrid Perpetual Roses and the Hybrid Teas, these three ancestral types fell into oblivion.

Other species of Eastern roses have also played roles, if less important ones, in the story of the rose, and deserve mention, if only for their beauty. The *Rosa banksiae,* arriving in Scotland in the late 18th century and named for the director of the Kew Gardens, Joseph Banks, is a climber of great strength. The white- or cream-colored varieties *normalis* and *lutescens* have single corollas, whereas *alba-plena* and *lutea* have double corollas. These roses continue to bless us with the grace typical of the Mediterranean or temperate-zoned gardens, where they are still cultivated.

The *Rosa multiflora,* a climber with great clusters of light-colored flowers, has played an important role in the creation of the corymb roses, the Floribunda. The *Rosa bracteata,* another Chinese climbing rose, also arrived in London during the late 18th century through the efforts of Lord MacCartney. It boasts splendid cedar-colored evergreen foliage and flat, snow-white flowers with heart-shaped petals. It has not been very prolific in producing descendants, but its hybrid 'Mermaid' is charming, though unfortunately only in temperate climates.

The *Rosa wichuraiana,* from China, Japan, and Korea, brought to Europe only at the end of the last century, is another climber, with an impetuous character. It exhibits the special trait of forming roots at every knot in the branches that crawl along the ground, with the "ramblers" borne from these roots being very beautiful.

Another rose worthy of mention is the *Rosa moyesii,* with its varieties 'Eos', 'Geranium', and 'Highdownensis'. These roses have small single flowers of short duration, though of a radiant, vivid color.

Finally, the *Rosa rugosa,* a sea-loving coastal plant that grows spontaneously (particularly along the coast of Japan) gave rise during the 19th century to numerous splendid mutations and varieties. Many gardens, along the American northern Atlantic seaboard and in Northern Europe particularly, still boast these varieties today.

The Golden Age of Roses

Old Acquaintances

Had we some kind of magic telescope that would enable us to look into an early 19th-century garden, we would probably find ourselves falling hopelessly in love with the roses we would discover, for they would seem so fluid and delicate—the very roses of which poets speak, those that are magnificent for but a single hour.

The roses from those times are old acquaintances, not only those roses cultivated in past centuries, but all the hybrids that have descended from them—the new varieties of *damask, gallica, alba,* and *centifolia.*

Standing out right away among the *damask* roses in that early garden would be 'Celsiana', an extremely seductive, silver-toned rose; 'Kazanlik', so fragrant as to be the choice in cultivations destined for the extraction of essences, such as those in Bulgaria; 'York and Lancaster', a mixture of red and white roses; 'Ispahan', with its Oriental charm; and 'Mme. Hardy', which some believe to be the most beautiful white rose of all time.

Let's move now to the *gallica,* always superbly beautiful. The Empress Josephine knew this rose well; she collected 167 varieties in the rosebed of Malmaison. In addition to the 'Empress Josephine' and 'Marie Luise', dedicated to Napoleon's two wives, and 'La Belle Sultane', violet-purple in color, a garden could not do without the *gallica complicata,* with her large, single, blazing pink corollas. Vibert, a famous hybridizer of that

Blush Noisette

time, presented us with the speckled 'Camaieux' and the Romantic 'Duchesse d'Angouleme'. But the reddest of the gallica, with a velvet glow that shades into black, was 'Tuscany Superb', a variant so old its origins are not known.

Then there are the *alba* roses: 'Maiden's Blush' (or 'Cuisse de Nymphe'), already mentioned in Turner's work; 'Celestial', truly worthy of the heavens; and 'Königin von Denmark', with its incredible geometrical interweaving of petals.

Last, but hardly least, are the *centifolia,* of which we have both old and new varieties. 'Reine des Centfeuilles' is one of the most classic and pompous. The muscosa were still few in number at the beginning of the 19th century and appeared later with the very beautiful 'Alfred de Dalmas'. 'Chapeau de Napoléon', more than with musk, is furnished with combs, and has a bud that is truly in the shape of a hat.

All appears sweet and calm in this ideal garden that we have admired from a distance. The roses bloom radiantly, wither away in the space of a morning, then reflower once again, not unaware of their own brevity and fleeting beauty. In fact, during the first half of the 19th century, the queen of flowers enjoyed some sensational moments. Three important groups of roses were about to make their triumphal entrances into European gardens: the Portland Roses, the Noisette Roses, and the Bourbon Roses. Not only did they establish themselves in cultivated gardens, they also announced the advent of a revolution that completely changed the world of the rose.

Portland Roses

During a trip to Italy, the Duchess of Portland noticed a brightly colored rose—brilliant scarlet—which flowered repeatedly, and she brought one back with her to England. Another of these rosebushes was sent to Monsieur Dupont, gardener to the Empress Josephine at Malmaison, at that time a center of interest for roses.

Named 'Duchess of Portland' in honor of its discoverer, this rose, which gave clear signs of having descended from a *chinensis* and a *damask* (with the probable intervention as well of a *gallica,* given the intensity of its color) became the object of much study. Before long a small group of varieties was obtained from seed cultivation or spontaneous mutation. The descendant with the highest quality, cultivated at St. Cloud in Louis XVIII's gardens, was a royal rose, 'La Rose du Roi', the "top seed" for generations of roses to come.

Noisette Roses

The second group is of less aristocratic origin, growing out of the passion of the two Noisette brothers: Philippe in Charleston, South Carolina, and Louis in Paris. Several rosebushes, which Philippe developed by crossing a Chinese (probably the 'Pink China' by Parson) with a *Rosa moschata,* crossed the ocean to Louis.

It took but a moment for these flowers to conquer Paris. 'Blush Noisette', a climber with pale pink flower clusters, acquired great fame. The same outcome awaited its descendants, including the 'Aimée Vibert', still much admired in the 20th century by the likes of Ellen Willmott, Gertrude Jekyll, and Graham Thomas, the greatest names among those who have written about and cultivated roses. Successive hybridizations with another of the stud roses, 'Yellow China' by Parks, produced the renowned yellow Noisettes 'Céline Forestier' and 'Maréchal Niel', with their unique golden-green color. It should not be forgotten that besides being roses that can boast repeating blooms, the Noisettes are very fragrant.

Bourbon Roses

The third group is that of the Bourbon Roses, perhaps the most important of the period. The Bourbons appeared at the same time as the Noisettes, around 1820. Several rosebush seedlings that grew in thick hedges on Bourbon Island (known today as Réunion) in the Indian Ocean were sent to Paris. They were thought to be Chinese roses similar to Parson's 'Pink China' and the autumn *damask.* When cultivated, they produced a new, splendid type of rose, with strong-scented, large flowers with full, globular corollas. Not least among their charms is that they were capable of reflowering.

The best Bourbon Roses, defined today as "antique roses," have lost nothing of their charm, and find their place in gardens next to other romantic roses such as those of David Austin. These include: 'Souvenir de la Malmaison', celestially glorious; 'Reine Victoria', truly Victorian in its opulence; and 'Bourbon Queen', which maintains the *damask*'s admirable corolla shape.

By the time the excellence of these three new types of roses was known, no one could stop the headlong rush among ambitious gardeners to develop the perfect rose. With so much fascinating horticultural raw material available, experimentation commenced with enthusiasm.

For the new cross-fertilizations the Portland Roses became available, in particular the 'Rose du Roi'; the

Reine des Violettes

Bourbons were also available; and continually joining the fray were the Chinese, as their fantastic reflowering was the element most sought after for transmission to descendants. But the game of chromosomes and genes holds many surprises, and when two roses are crossed, roses that are themselves offspring of many crosses, it is not easy to predict which traits will come through. With the passage of time and continual crossings for excellent traits, the classes that define different rose types lose their definition, and more and more roses will defy the classification schemes known today.

Hybrid Perpetual Roses

Toward the middle of the 19th century a new type of rose, the result of much painstaking and patient effort, made its appearance. The honor of officially representing this new type went to the 'Rose de la Reine', created by Laffay in 1842 in the French town of Auteuil.

This type of rose was named Hybrid Reflowering in France and Hybrid Perpetual in England. The name of these vigorous and very fragrant shrubs clearly emphasizes their reflowering. We shouldn't be surprised that the Perpetual or Reflowering roses, however we choose to call them, became the most sought-after, most cultivated, and most frequent roses in competitions all through the rest of the 19th century until the arrival of the Hybrid Teas. The Perpetual roses are pleasing for their abundance and also the size of their flowers, which is usually considerable, and for their intense fragrance and great rusticity. Some acquired such fame that we know them today by the same names: 'Paul Neyron' (from 1869), 'Docteur Jamain', 'Reine des Violettes', and, above all, the late-arriving 'Frau Karl Druschki' (from 1901), still found today in many gardens.

The Hybrid Perpetual thus became the uncontested champion of the gardens. However, the road that led horticulturists to that point certainly had not ended. New objectives were as enticing as those just achieved, and they involved new combinations among the emerging groups. One of the persistent objectives was to marry a robust, rustic, and vigorous race, rich in scent, such as the Perpetual Roses, with a more delicate, elegant, and refined race, such as the Tea Roses. The result of this marriage was the Hybrid Tea Roses.

Modern Roses

The Hybrid Tea Rose

The complicated work of hybridization and selection— roses are at times resistant to marriage—to develop Hybrid Teas was undertaken during the second half of the 19th century. However, the Hybrid Tea Rose belongs entirely to this century.

The names connected with the Hybrid Teas are those of Guillot, whose rose 'La France' was ordained in 1867 as the first Hybrid Tea Rose (even though the official recognition of this category occurred later during the 1890s); and that of the Englishman Henry Bennett, to whom we owe the more scientific organization and stricter control of the hybridization work. In fact, from Bennett we have the first group of Hybrid Teas that are furnished with every date of their origin. A third name is that of Pernet Ducher, father of the Pernettiane Roses. Thanks to the crosses carried out by this French horticulturist with Persian roses, the *Rosa foetida* and *foetida bicolor,* the color yellow and all its shades became part of the Hybrid Teas' spectrum.

From the end of last century, beginning with the highly popular 'Mme. Caroline Testout' (also by Pernet Ducher and cultivated and widespread in thousands of specimens) until today, the creation of new hybrids in all corners of the world has known little lapse.

Increased scientific knowledge about the sexuality of plants, the progress of hybridization techniques, and instruments such as the microscope have gradually led the rose's potential to reach its fullest expression. The Hybrid Teas today represent the dominant group of roses, dominant in terms of their ubiquity and prestige.

The Hybrid Teas have large flowers that are perpetual, and though most appear in shrub form, climbing varieties are also known.

Polyantha and Floribunda Roses

The Floribunda, together with the Hybrid Teas, are the roses most cultivated in the 20th century. The numerous Floribunda have been grouped together by botanists after various developments and a series of rather complicated passages. This family of shrub rose is no higher than about thirty-five inches, and has flowers united in large clusters with lengthy and abundant reflowering.

Floribunda Roses stem from a spontaneous cross between *Rosa multiflora* and two of her descendants, 'Paquerette' and 'Mignonette'. *Rosa multiflora* is a climber of Asian origin with large panicles of small, gay, cream-colored flowers. 'Paquerette' and 'Mignonette' are dwarf Chinese roses from Guillot's nurseries in Lyons. The small group of rosebushes that emerged from further selection work was first named Polypom, and then changed to Dwarf Polyantha in the early 20th century when botanists identified two hundred cultivars having traits sufficiently similar to justify the birth of a new class.

Dwarf Polyanthas are short rosebushes, with small, very often double, flowers. Though they were exceptionally popular when first developed, they were destined to be overshadowed. After 1920, Dines Poulsen in Denmark turned his attention to a new series of cross-fertilizations between the Polyanthas and the Hybrid Teas, thereby developing the umpteenth race of roses with larger flowers, many of which bear his name. The Poulsen Roses attracted the attention of other horticulturists, and as had occurred with the Hybrid Teas, there began a frenzied production of this type of rose. At first called Hybrid Polyanthas and later renamed Floribunda, the world's greatest cultivators competed in producing these roses: first Le Grice, followed by Dickson, Harkness, Kordes, and Tantau; among the Americans, Lammerts, Boerner, and Swim. After the 1970s new names also appeared: Warriner, for example, and the Japanese.

The versatility of the Floribunda Roses, their abundance, their ease of cultivation and placement, and their excellent use in a decorative role assured that there would be uninterrupted production to meet the ever-increasing demand. Today there are hundreds and hundreds of Floribunda varieties.

Miniature Roses

Another type of Modern Rose that has had success during the last thirty years, thanks to their ease of cultivation and placement, and their resistance and strength, are the Miniature Roses.

The Miniatures derive from a Chinese rose, the *Rosa chinensis minima* which, back in the 19th century, had produced several interesting offspring, such as the 'Pompon de Paris'. But it was only around the middle of the 20th century, thanks primarily to the work of hybridizers such as the Spaniard Pedro Dot, the American Robert Pyle, and the Dutchman Jan de Vink, that a series of cultivars was created that was greatly successful. Today these varieties, produced by almost all the largest rose enterprises, are very numerous and also include the climbing and mossy Miniatures.

Even though rosebushes with taller and larger flowers are sometimes listed pell-mell in this category, the true Miniature, as its name indicates, is very small-sized; the shrubs are no higher than about fifteen inches, with minute foliage and equally miniscule, though perfect, roses.

Shrub Roses

Under this name (in French it is *Rosiers Arbustes,* in German *Strauchrosen*) the present classification groups together all those roses larger in size than a Hybrid Tea or other roses in shrub form, and whose more upright growth and less uniform and compact shape make them unsuitable for flowerbeds. While a bushy rose or a Hybrid Tea is allowed at most a height of one and one-half yards, a shrub rose may attain two yards, with curved and sometimes wandering branches, almost like those of a climber.

Some texts list both old roses and modern ones that conform to the above-mentioned traits among the shrub roses. Others prefer to separate out all the roses created in this century and, though keeping for each of these the family name that defines their lineage, to define them simply and generically as "Old Garden Roses."

In this large and heterogeneous company we thus find isolated roses that do not belong to any group, or roses that present the typical traits of the family head from which they are descended, such as hybrids from the *Rosa rugosa* hybrids, the *Rosa muscosa,* or the *Rosa eglanteria.*

Max Graf

Groundcover Roses

The use of rosebushes as groundcover plants is not at all improper, since several species in their natural state crawl along the ground, spreading out and covering whatever they encounter along the way. Examples are the *Rosa wichuraiana*, the *Rosa luciae*, the *Rosa bracteata*, and to a lesser degree, the European *Rosa arvensis*.

The arrival from America in 1919 of 'Max Graf' excited interest in the creation of roses destined for this use; the mantling roses create very pleasing effects, especially along sloping terrain. Allowed to run freely wherever it desires, 'Max Graf', halfway between a rosebush and a climber, spreads out to form a large wheel, and its bright corollas nestle among the leaves like field flowers. Very notable is the *R. bracteata*, which flattens itself on the ground with piles of bold, evergreen, glossy-glimmering leaves. It is also excellent for checking erosion, but can be quite invasive if allowed to grow unattended.

Various rosebushes available over the past thirty years can easily work as groundcover plants. One popular example is the prodigiously reflowering "Sea Foam', a small, luxuriant shrub that has won three awards, including a gold medal at Rome in 1963. 'Sea Foam' fulfills the promise of her name with light-colored clusters of pompon-shaped corollas that look like snow-white foam covering an emerald-green sea.

Also adapted for this use are other roses that are aptly called carpet, blanket, cushion, spray, or even wave. Examples include 'Rosy Cushion', 'Red Blanket' (Dickson, 1979), 'Pink Wave' (Mattock, 1983), 'Tapis Volant', 'Pink Spray', and 'White Spray', all by Lens. We also add Poulsen's little bells, 'Pink Bells' and 'Red Bells', Kordes's 'Grouse', and Suzuki's 'Ferdy'. Meilland's creeping plants are many in number and differ in height and vigor. Notable examples include 'Fiona' and 'Candy Rose'. The Japanese 'Nozomi', a Miniature, is among the best candidates for covering a few square yards of stripped land, or for growing over low walls.

Speaking of height, we should make clear that not all the roses mentioned above, like 'Max Graf' and 'Nozomi', are truly low-lying and creeping. 'Red Blanket' and 'Rosy Cushion', for example, rise up to nearly three feet before growing in width; others are simply small and shrubby, with a tendency to grow wider.

Climbers and Ramblers

Several wild roses feature long and vigorous branches, or sarmentums, which may reach up to a height of three or four yards and, in the case of some Chinese roses, even as high as fifteen or twenty yards. These roses are called climbers. They are used in gardens to cover buildings, arbors or pavilions, or to make trellislike, green walls. Climbing roses can serve to separate various areas of the garden, or they can rise up as flowering columns amid the green of meadows.

Climbing roses attracted the attention of hybridizers in the last century, but it wasn't until the 20th century that many varieties, originating from different species, became incorporated into gardens and parks.

Climbing roses are divided into two categories, each having distinct characteristics and uses. One category includes those climbers with stiff, strong stems and large, reflowering corollas. The second category are the ramblers, which are more highly developed and much richer in foliage, with small flowers in large clusters that are generally not reflowering. Among climbers, the choice ranges from single rosebushes, which do not belong to any special class, to the climbing forms that derive from the Hybrid Teas, the Reflowering Hybrids, the Floribunda, and the Miniatures. Among the ramblers, on the other hand, it is the *Rosa wichuraiana* that offers a valuable selection of varieties.

The information contained in the rose descriptions throughout this book includes: the name of the rose, synonyms (if any), the name of the creator, registration data, origin, description of the flower and plant, and awards.

The × that appears in some cases between the genus and species indicates the hybrid origin from a spontaneous or planned cross between two species.

The term sport *indicates genetic mutation that results in the change of a particular characteristic, for example, the petal color or the "bearing" of the plant.*

Frau Karl Druschki

Hybrid Perpetual Roses

Around 1820 the rose world was celebrating the arrival of the lovely Noisette and the sumptuous Bourbon. After 1830, it witnessed the appearance of another group of roses with a more complicated origin, destined to have sweeping success. These roses were the result of a web of marriages in which early participants were the 'Rose du Roi' (a direct descendant of that famous rose discovered in Italy by the Duchess of Portland), Chinese reflowering hybrids, and eventually even the Noisettes and the Bourbons themselves. Entering the fray later on were the Teas. In truth, the hybridizers' efforts involved every available rose. The results were not always satisfying, and many roses enjoyed only fleeting glory. The date that consecrates the advent of this new type is 1842, when the horticulturist Laffay created 'La Rose de la Reine', lilac-pink with cup-shaped corollas like those of a *centifolia*.

The terms by which these newest hybrids came to be defined in the two countries most interested in their production and cultivation, 'Hybrides Remontantes' and 'Hybrid Perpetuals', are quite appropriate and get at the most obvious quality of these roses—their reflowering. Hybrids they certainly were, much more so than people were used to in those days, and they certainly flowered repeatedly. Furthermore, the best of these roses could consistently produce large corollas, an intense fragrance, great strength, and resistance to extreme cold.

These excellent qualities contributed to the great popularity of these hybrid roses. They became the main attraction of the flower shows and competitions that were so highly fashionable during the second half of the 19th century in the elegant Parisian and Victorian circles. By 1878 there were already 538 cultivars. France became the leading country for their production, asin the case of the Bourbons and Noisettes. The names of the most important creators were Laffay of Auteuil and Sisley of Lyon. The colors varied from white to rose, crimson, purple, and violet. Other shades had to await later crosses with the Teas, which, in addition to further increasing the reflowerings, also sensibly changed the shape of the corollas and design of the petals.

Up until the first years of the 20th century, when they began their decline, many Reflowering Hybrid Roses (both shrub-form and climbers) were the rage, acquiring great fame undimmed by time. Posterity has been presented with 'Paul Neyron', red as blood, from 1869; 'Docteur Jamain', prune colored; 'Baronne Adolphe de Rothschild', extremely attractive; 'Reine de Violettes', with petals delicately creased and a charming violet tip; and 'General Jacqueminot', scarlet-crimson with strong Bourbon traits and a strong damask fragrance. Among the last were the pale 'Frau Karl Druschki', created by Peter Lambert in 1901 and considered by many to be the most beautiful German rose, and 'Ferdinand Pichard', with its soft specklings.

BARON GIROD DE L'AIN

by Reverchon, 1897. Parentage: sport of 'Eugène Fürst'. Brilliant red corollas edged in white.

BARONNE ADOLPHE DE ROTHSCHILD

('Baroness Rothschild') by Pernet Pere, 1868. Parentage: sport of 'Souvenir de la Reine d'Angleterre'. Vigorous, erect; partially perpetual; large cup-shaped corollas of 40 petals, delicate red-tinted white.

CAPTAIN HAYWARD

by Bennett, 1893. Parentage: seedling of 'Triomphe de l'Exposition'. Vigorous, occasionally perpetual; large corollas of 25 petals, turbinate, clear crimson with clear edges, large, orange fruit. Fragrant.

EUGÈNE FÜRST

by Soupert & Notting, 1875. Parentage: 'Baron de Bonstetten' × unknown. Perpetual; large corollas, full and globular, crimson-shaded with purple. Fragrant.

FERDINAND PICHARD

by Tanne, 1921. Tall, vigorous; perpetual; double corollas of 25 petals, striped red and scarlet, yellow stamens.

FRAU KARL DRUSCHKI

('Reine des Neiges', 'Snow Queen', 'White American Beauty') by P. Lambert, 1901. Parentage: 'Merveille de Lyon' × 'Mme. Caroline Testout'. Vigorous; large corollas of 35 petals, snow-white sometimes with a pale pink center, pointed buds, carmine-red tints, dark leaves. No fragrance.

GÉNÉRAL JACQUEMINOT

('General Jack', 'Jack Rose') by Roussel, 1853. Parentage: probably a seedling of 'Gloire de Rosomanes'. Vigorous, bushy; perpetual; typical hybrid perpetual. Corollas of 27 petals carried by long, rigid steles, dark red with clear underside, intense green leaves. Very fragrant.

GLOIRE DE CHÉDANE-GUINOISEAU

by Chédane-Pajotin, 1907. Parentage: 'Gloire de Ducher' × unknown variety. Vigorous, occasionally perpetual; large corollas of 40 petals, cup-shaped, beautiful form, dark, soft leaves. Fragrant.

Baron Girod de l'Ain

Baronne Adolphe de Rothschild

Captain Hayward

Ferdinand Pichard

Eugène Fürst

Général Jacqueminot

Frau Karl Druschki

Gloire de Chédane-Guinoisseau

Gloire de Ducher

Mme. Albert Barbier

Granny Grimmett's

Mrs. John Laing

Oskar Cordel

Henry Nevard

Prince Camille de Rohan

Rashomon

Reine des Violettes

Roger Lambelin

GLOIRE DE DUCHER
by Ducher, 1865. Occasionally perpetual; very large and full corollas, dark red. Fragrant.

GRANNY GRIMMETT'S
Creator and parentage unknown. Corollas of 25 petals, purple-violet.

HENRY NEVARD
by F. Cant, 1924. Parentage unknown. Vigorous, bushy; perpetual; very large, cup-shaped corollas of 30 petals, crimson-scarlet, dark, coriaceous leaves. Very fragrant.

MME. ALBERT BARBIER
by Barbier, 1925. Parentage: 'Frau Karl Druschki' × unknown. Vigorous, bushy; perpetual; large, cup-shaped corollas of 50 petals, salmon-tinted yellow with darker center. Slightly fragrant.

MRS. JOHN LAING
by Bennett, 1887. Parentage: 'François Michelon' × unknown. Vigorous, dwarf; perpetual; large corollas of 45 petals, pointed buds, light leaves. Fragrant.

OSKAR CORDEL
by P. Lambert, 1897. Parentage: 'Merveille de Lyon' × 'André Schwartz'. Vigorous, compact; large, cup-shaped corollas of 40 petals. Fragrant.

PRINCE CAMILLE DE ROHAN
('La Rosière') by E. Verdier, 1861. Parentage: probably a hybrid of 'Générale Jacqueminot' × 'Géant des Batailles'. Vigorous, erect; sometimes perpetual; large corollas, many doubles on weak steles, crimson-velvet brown. Very fragrant.

RASHOMON
Creator and parentage unknown. Corollas of 50 petals, deep pink centers with white outside. Fragrant.

REINE DES VIOLETTES
('Queen of the Violets') by Millet-Malet, 1860. Parentage: seedling of 'Pius IX'. Perpetual; large corollas of 75 petals, violet-purple, sparse leaves. Very fragrant.

ROGER LAMBELIN
by Vve Schwartz, 1890. Parentage: sport of 'Fisher Holmes'. Vigorous; perpetual; irregularly-shaped corollas of 30 petals, curled crimson that turns brown with white edges.

Tea Roses and Tea Rose Hybrids

All the roses grouped together today in the large family of the Tea Rose Hybrids descend mainly from several Chinese roses, but the story here is not entirely clear. They apparently descend from the *Rosa chinensis* and the *Rosa gigantea,* and from crosses between these two species. These roses are said to have a tealike scent, one similar to that which escapes from a just-opened box of good tea. However, this scent is purely legendary since, although old documents speak of it, no one has ever smelled it in any of the Tea Roses that have descended from the originals. The Tea Roses are nevertheless highly scented with slightly differing fragrances.

Ancient images from the Orient testify to the early existence of the *Rosa chinensis,* but the Chinese roses became known in Europe only much later. Several are depicted in texts belonging to the Linnaeus collection from the early part of the 18th century. It is said that a Chinese rose was grown in 1750 in the Chelsea Physic Gardens, and another at Kew.

Nevertheless, it was four important Chinese roses that changed the destiny and history of the rose in Europe and the world, and they are referenced as the stud China roses. Imported to Europe between 1792 and 1824, and crossed with the roses that were then being cultivated in gardens, the stud China roses gave rise to all the modern roses.

In particular, two of these roses were the progenitors of what are today called Tea Rose Hybrids. One reached Europe in 1810 and was sent by an agent of the English East India Company to Mr. Abraham Hume of London. From then on authors referred to it as the 'Hume's Blush Tea-scented China'. It was wonderfully scented and had the same delicate pink color of a timid girl's flushed cheek.

Four years later 'Park's Yellow Tea-scented China' arrived, sent this time to Mr. John Dampier Parks, a collector of rare plants for the Royal Horticultural Society. This was immortalized by Redouté in his wonderful work "Les Roses" under the name of *Rosa sulphurea.* Its color was yellow, a fact of some importance, since up until that time there were no yellow roses to be found in gardens.

A number of gardeners, many of them French, began to work assiduously on these two roses. The Chinese roses, in addition to the splendid form of their corollas with elongated petals, possessed an enviable quality: exceptional reflowering, lasting throughout the season. Of the Western roses, only autumn's *damascena* could flower twice a year.

It wasn't long before the first Tea Roses were born. However, the story of these initial years of feverish cross-fertilization is not known. Only 'Safrano' is of certain genealogy and was created in 1839 by Beauregard in France. The 'Safrano' can be given the title of Europe's first Tea Rose.

The Tea Roses were delicate roses; they suffered from the cold and had a frail constitution. Beautiful on account of their thin, pointed buds and pastel shades, they were very elegant but not very hardy. They certainly were well suited to the aristocratic gardens of that period, but it was very unlikely that they would satisfy the tastes of the larger and less-refined public that was becoming increasingly fond of roses. This public sought plants that were more vigorous and could be cultivated elsewhere than just along the Riviera or in greenhouses. They wanted brighter and bolder colors that would stand out.

Faced with these needs, horticulturists responded

with the Tea Rose Hybrids, a type of rose obtained by crossing the Tea Roses with the vigorous Perpetual Rose Hybrids, the rose most commonly grown in Europe in the second half of the 19th century. The history of the rose is contained in the patient, untiring, and even maniacal work of a few truly dedicated souls. Furnished with brushes for carrying the pollen from one plant to the pistil of another, these perfectionists cultivated, nursed, and waited, hoping to create eventually plants that possessed all the imaginable and desirable qualities —the perfect rose.

In fact, the new hybrids did possess extraordinary virtues: from the Perpetual Hybrid Roses they obtained strength, vigor, and resistance to cold; from the Tea Roses elegance, sweetness of scent, great color variety, and a beautifully shaped flower and bud.

The official birth of the first Hybrid Tea Rose was in 1867, created by Guillot and called 'La France'. During the 19th century, reproduction techniques had not yet been perfected, nor were the rose specialists very meticulous; Guillot was unable to say precisely how he had produced his rose.

Selection became more controlled, and the hybridization program more precise and scientific through the work of the Englishman Henry Bennett. It was Bennett who established that each rose should have its own "pedigree," a sort of identity card listing the names of the roses used in the cross-fertilization and the year and place of its birth. He did much for the creation and diffusion of an early group of Tea Hybrids. One of these which enjoyed great success was the 'Lady Mary Fitzwilliam', a very fertile rosebush often used as a parent by several other hybridizers.

An important event in the history of the Tea Rose Hybrids was the arrival in the family of the first truly yellow roses. The father of the yellow roses is Pernet-Ducher, another French horticulturist. He strengthened the color of the Tea Roses by using *Rosa foetida* and *Rosa foetida bicolor* in the cross-fertilization. These Persian roses were the yellowest roses then in existence. His efforts were crowned with success, and in 1900 Pernet-Ducher presented the world with his 'Soleil d'Or', followed in 1910 by the 'Rayon d'Or', both charmingly pure yellow in color. Other important roses that remain tied to the name of Pernet-Ducher are 'Mme. Caroline Testout' and 'Antoine Rivoire'.

The Tea Rose Hybrids marched triumphantly through the 20th century, constantly searching for new colors, increasingly satisfying corolla shapes, and greater vigor and resistance to cold and disease. Their beauty was so perfect that nearly every other type of rose disappeared from our gardens. With novelty upon novelty, hundreds of Tea Hybrids were introduced, competed, awarded prizes, and cultivated.

Many of these roses are today found only as names in books, important stages in the history of the rose, perhaps, but no longer present in our gardens. Others are timeless, and remain with us along with the most recent novelties.

Many of these "historical" roses, whether they are cultivated today or not, remain alive and glorious in memory. One of the first in this pantheon of roses was 'Ophelia', by William Paul in 1912. These roses were superb in shape and rich in scent, and had two splendid mutations, 'Mme. Butterfly' and 'Lady Silvia'.

'Mme. Butterfly', cultivated in thousands of specimens, was presented to the world by Gurney Hill of the United States, which by the beginning of the century was already in competition with Europe for the production of roses. By 1920 there were already 114 American Tea Hybrids, among them the famous 'General McArthur' and 'Los Angeles' by Fred H. Howard.

In the 1920s came the success of the Irish, chiefly of Dickson ('Shot Silk' and 'Dame Edith Helen') and of McGredy. Several of the latter's roses, known for their tenuous color shades, bear the family name, as in 'McGredy Yellow', 'McGredy Ivory', and 'Margaret McGredy'. 'Crimson Glory' by Kordes was very famous in 1935 and received an award for its scent.

The war years were as dark for the world of roses as they were for mankind. After this painful pause, dilettantes began to attract attention. Albert Norman assured himself of two gold medals with 'Ena Harkness', dedicated to an Englishman who would soon become a great hybridizer; and Charles Mallerin, a former railway man, created 'Virgo'.

The ascendency of Meilland of Antibes began in 1945 with the introduction of 'Peace'. This rose spread throughout the world in millions of specimens, and for a time it almost became a living symbol of peace and brotherhood among men. In 1946 it was the turn of the radiant 'Michèle Meilland', followed by 'Eden Rose', 'Bettina', 'Baccarà', 'Maria Callas', and 'Pharaoh'. 'Youki-San', a gold-medal-winner at Baden Baden, was one of the few scented white Tea Hybrids.

The successes during the 1950s and 1960s are too many to number; the requests for new roses became crushing. Entering the "hall of fame" were 'Sutter's Gold' by Swim and 'Kordes' Perfecta' by Kordes, which spread across America with thousands of specimens planted in Portland, Oregon. Also entering the fray were 'Wendy Cussons' by Gregory, winner of five medals,

Tantau's incandescent 'Super Star', and Lens's white 'Pascali'. During the same period success returned to the Dickson enterprise with 'Grandpa Dickson', 'Red Devil', and 'Bonsoir'.

From the 1970s we have 'Just Joey' by Cants of Colchester, with its bright-colored, rippling petals; 'Double Delight' by Swim, winner of four awards including a gold at Rome; and the charming 'Silver Jubilee', dedicated by Cocker to the twenty-fifth anniversary of Queen Elizabeth's reign.

During the 1980s the Meilland establishment continued to roar, with 'Cathérine Deneuve', 'Luis de Funès', 'Meizeli', and 'Madame Fernandel'. Movie stars have taken the place of queens and duchesses in providing names for roses: For Poulsen, 'Ingrid Bergman' stands out. Some roses first appear with simple, odd-sounding acronyms with the initial letters indicating the first part of the firm's name: 'Meitixia', 'Dickput', and 'Keisfult' (all given awards at Monza in 1985).

New names have begun to make headway among the hybridizers. On everyone's lips in the United States are 'Summer Dream' and 'Silhouette' by Warriner, while the Japanese roses increasingly receive awards at the expense of their Western counterparts. Suzuki has given us 'Kan-pai' and, in 1985 Kaichiro Ota produced 'Lucky Choice'. At the same time that 'Jardins de Bagatelle' was received in France, the Italians and Spanish were making strides: Barni presented 'Annabella'; Embriaco, 'Patrice';

Cazzaniga, 'Sorriso di Pace'; and Dot, 'Ljuba Rizzoli'.

A Tea Hybrid is expected to have a perfect flower form, extending from a long and rigid stem with a pair of buds. Although there are a few beautiful Tea Rose Hybrids with single flowers, such as 'Dainty Bess', 'White Wings', and 'Mrs. Oakley Fischer', almost all have full, rich, and striking corollas.

We can expect to find these roses in all colors except blue—for which rose cultivators have fought in vain, getting only so far as mauve. All the other hues are present. One can find the coral rose, the peach rose, the porcelain rose, the shell-colored rose; the salmon, ocher, honey, and amber rose; the pure white, ivory, and cream-colored rose; the currant-red, blood-red, and nearly black, velvety red rose. And then there are the bicolored flowers, with one color for the underside of the petal and another for the inside of the petal: pink and silver, gold and vermillion, yellow and orange, cream and scarlet.

With Tea Rose Hybrids one can expect a long flowering period, followed by a second that is shorter but nevertheless substantial. These roses vary tremendously in quality regarding growth, strength, and hardiness. Something we should not always expect to find is fragrance; after all the passages, crosses, bunglings, and manipulations, the fragrance has often been lost—a penalty, as it were, to be paid in exchange for such beauty.

AKAMIKADO
Creator and parentage unknown.

DUCHESSE DE BRABANT
('Comtesse de Labarthe', 'Comtesse Ouwaroff') by Bernède,
1857. Parentage unknown. Vigorous and wide; large,
cup-shaped corollas of 45 petals, delicate rose color. Very
fragrant.

LADY HILLINGDON
by Lowe & Shawyer, 1910. Parentage: 'Papa Gontier' ×
'Mme. Hoste.' Bushy, somewhat rustic; semidouble corollas,
yellow-apricot color, tapered and pointed buds, bronze leaves.
Fragrant.

NIPHETOS
by Bougère, 1843. Greenhouse variety, once very popular;
spherical corollas. Very fragrant.

SAFRANO
by Beauregard, 1839. Vigorous; large, semidouble corollas,
yellow apricot and yellow saffron in color, pointed buds.
Fragrant.

SNOWFLAKE
('Marie Lambert', 'White Hermosa'), by E. Lambert,
1886. Parentage: Sport of 'Mme. Bravy'.

SOUVENIR D'UN AMI
by Bélot-Defougère, 1846. Vigorous; double, cup-shaped
corollas, very large, pale rose color with salmon highlights.
Very fragrant.

WHITE DUCHESSE DE BRABANT
('Mme. Joseph Schwartz') by J. Schwartz, 1880.
Parentage: Probably a sport of 'Duchesse de Brabant'.
Vigorous; medium corollas, full form, white with scarlet-red
highlights.

Akamikado

Duchesse de Brabant

Lady Hillingdon

Snowflake

Niphetos

Souv. d'un Ami

Safrano

White Duchesse de Brabant

Aalsmeer Gold

Akebono

Adolf Horstmann

Aenne Burda

AALSMEER GOLD
('Bekola') by Kordes, 1978. Parentage: 'Berolina' ×
seedling. Vigorous and erect, bushy growth; corollas of 23
petals, long buds, tapered, glossy leaves. Slightly fragrant.

ADOLF HORSTMANN
by R. Kordes, 1971. Parentage: 'Colour Wonder' × 'Dr.
A. J. Verhange'. Upright, vigorous; classic corolla form,
large, double, glossy leaves. Slightly fragrant.

AENNE BURDA
by Kordes, 1971. Vigorous, upright and bushy growth;
large, double corollas, large, glossy leaves. Slightly fragrant.

AKEBONO
by Kawai, 1964. Parentage: 'Ethel Sanday' × 'Narzisse'.
Vigorous and upright; large corollas of 56 petals, pointed,
pale yellow flushed carmine, dark, glossy leaves.

ALEC'S RED
('Cored') by Cocker, 1973. Parentage: 'Fragrant Cloud' ×
'Dame de Coeur'. Vigorous and upright; large corollas of 45
petals, opaque leaves. Fragrant. Gold Medal, Royal
National Rose Society, 1970.

Alec's Red

ALEXANDRA

('Alexander', 'Harlex') by Harkness, 1972. Parentage: 'Tropicana' × ('Ann Elizabeth' × 'Allgold'). Tall and vigorous; corollas of 25 petals, very large, tapered buds, glossy leaves. Slightly fragrant. Gold Medal, Belfast, 1974.

ALLEGRO 80

('Meifikalif') by M. L. Meilland, 1980. Parentage: ('Diorette' × 'Tropicana') × (seedling × ('Diorette' × 'Tropicana')). Greenhouse variety; corollas of 35 petals. No fragrance.

ALPINE SUNSET

by Cants of Colchester, 1974. Parentage: 'Dr. A. J. Verhage' × 'Irish Gold'. Upright and vigorous; large, fragrant corollas of 30 petals, peach-pink with apricot reverse, glossy leaves.

ALTESSE

by F. Meilland, 1950. Parentage: 'Vercors' × 'Léonce Colombier'. Large, well-formed corollas, intense red.

ALTESSE '75

by Meilland, 1975. Well-formed corollas, 30 petals, pale yellow bordered in pale rose, becoming red in bloom.

AMATSU-OTOME

by Teranishi, 1960. Parentage: 'Chrysler Imperial' × 'Doreen'. Compact growth; large corollas, yellow with orange edges, cupped. Slightly fragrant.

AMBASSADOR

('Meinuzeten') by Meilland, 1979. Parentage: seedling × 'Whisky Mac'. Cupped corollas of 33 petals, orange-red with golden yellow reverse, conical buds, dark and glossy leaves.

AMBOSSFUNKEN

('Anvil Sparks') by Meyer, 1961. Dense bushy growth; large, well-formed corollas of 33 petals, coral streaked with gold. Fragrant.

Alexandra

Allegro '80

Alpine Sunset

Altesse

Ambassador

Altesse '75

Ambossfunken

Amatsu-Otome

AMERICANA
by Boerner, 1961. Parentage: 'Poinsettia' seedling × 'New Yorker'. Upright and vigorous; large corollas of 28 petals, ovoid buds, coriaceous leaves. Fragrant.

AMERICAN HERITAGE
('Lamlam') by Lammerts, 1965. Parentage: 'Queen Elizabeth' × 'Yellow Perfection'. Tall; double corollas, ivory and salmon blend, long buds, dark, coriaceous leaves. All-America Rose Selections Award, 1966.

AMERICAN PRIDE
by Warriner, 1974. Tall and upright; corollas of 33 petals, pointed buds, dark leaves. Slightly fragrant.

ANDRÉE JOUBERT
by Mallerin, 1952. Parentage: 'Soeur Thérèse' × 'Duquesa de Peñaranda'. Large, well-formed corollas, coral-orange.

ANGELIQUE
('Ankori', 'Korangeli') by Kordes, 1979. Parentage: 'Mercedes' × seedling. Bushy growth; well-formed corollas of 40 petals, large opaque leaves, medium green. Slightly fragrant.

ANN FACTOR
by Ellis & Swim, 1975. Parentage: 'Duet' × 'Jack O'Lantern'. Compact, vigorous shrub; very double corollas, first turbinate then cupped, bronzy, glossy, coriaceous leaves. Very fragrant.

ANN LETTS
by G. F. Letts & Sons, 1953. Parentage: 'Peace' × 'Charles Gregory'. Semidouble corollas, pink with reverse silvery, dark leaves; very spiny. Light, sweet fragrance.

ANTONIA RIDGE
('Meiparadon') by Paolino, 1976. Parentage: ('Chrysler Imperial' × 'Karl Herbst') × seedling. Large corollas of 30 petals. Slightly fragrant.

AOZORA
('Blue Sky') by Suzuki, 1973. Parentage: 'Sterling Silver' seedling × seedling. Upright; large double corollas, large coriaceous leaves. Fragrant.

Americana

American Heritage

American Pride

Andrée Joubert

Ann Letts

Angelique

Antonia Ridge

Ann Factor

Aozora

Apollo

Arizona

Ardelle

Arlene Francis

Aquarius

Asagumo

APOLLO
('Armolo') by D. L. Armstrong, 1971. Parentage: 'High Time' × 'Imperial Gold'. Upright and bushy; double corollas, long, pointed buds, dark, coriaceous leaves. Fragrant. All-America Rose Selections Award, 1972.

AQUARIUS
('Armaq') by E. L. Armstrong, 1971. Parentage: ('Charlotte Armstrong' × ('Fandango' × ('World's Fair' × 'Floradora'))). Vigorous, upright and bushy, disease resistant; ovoid buds, medium corollas, double rose shadings, large, coriaceous leaves. Slightly fragrant. Classified also among the Grandiflora. Gold medal Geneva, 1970, and All-America Rose Selections Award, 1971.

ARDELLE
by Eddie, Harkness & Wyant, 1957. Parentage: 'Mrs. Charles Lamplough' × 'Peace'. Large corollas of 50–60 petals, yellow shading into white. Fragrant.

ARIZONA
('Werina', 'Tocade') by Weeks, 1975. Parentage: (('Fred Howard' × 'Golden Scepter') × 'Golden Rapture') × (('Fred Howard' × 'Golden Scepter') × 'Golden Rapture'). Upright and dense growth; double corollas, bronze color, ovoid buds, dark, coriaceous leaves. Very fragrant. All-America Rose Selections Award, 1975.

ARLENE FRANCIS
by Boerner, 1957. Parentage: 'Eclipse' seedling × 'Golden Scepter'. Vigorous; large corollas of 30 petals, dark, coriaceous leaves. Very fragrant.

ASAGUMO
('Oriental Dawn') by Suzuki, 1973. Parentage: 'Peace' seedling × 'Charleston' seedling. Vigorous and upright; large and double corollas, globular, ovoid buds, glossy, dark leaves. Fragrant.

Athena

Atoll

Autumn

Ave Maria

ATHENA
('Rühkor') by W. Kordes, 1981. Parentage: seedling ×
'Helmut Schmidt'. Greenhouse variety, compact and upright;
corollas of 35 petals, large, opaque, medium green leaves.

ATOLL
('Clarita', 'Meybister') by Meilland, 1971. Parentage:
'Tropicana' × ('Zambra' × 'Romantica'). Upright and
very vigorous; large corollas of 33 petals, dark, opaque leaves.

AUTUMN
by Coddington, 1928. Parentage: 'Sensation' × 'Souvenir
de Claudius Pernet'. Very double corollas, cupped, orange
streaked red, dark, glossy leaves. Fragrant.

AVE MARIA
('Korav', 'Sunburnt Country') by W. Kordes, 1981.
Parentage: 'Uwe Seeler' × 'Sonia'. Upright, with small
prickles; corollas of 35 petals, large, fragrant.

AVENTURE
('Adventure') by P. Croix, 1965. Parentage: ('Corail' ×
'Baccará') × seedling. Vigorous, upright, and compact; large
corollas of 55 petals, coriaceous, glossy leaves.

Aventure

AVON

by Morey, 1961. Parentage: 'Nocturne' × 'Chrysler Imperial'. Large corollas of 23 petals, coriaceous leaves. Very fragrant.

AZTEC

by Swim, 1957. Parentage: 'Charlotte Armstrong' × seedling. Vigorous, spreading growth; large corollas of 25 petals, coriaceous, glossy leaves. Fragrant.

BACCARÁ

('Meger') by F. Meilland, 1954. Parentage: 'Happiness' × 'Independence'. Upright and bushy; medium-sized corollas, very double, 75 petals, cupped to flat, dark, coriaceous leaves.

BAJAZZO

by R. Kordes, 1961. Vigorous, upright; large corollas, well-formed, velvety red, reverse white. Very fragrant.

BEAUTÉ

by C. Mallerin, 1953. Parentage: 'Mme. Joseph Perraud' × seedling. Vigorous; well-formed corollas, large and double, tapered buds. Fragrant. Certificate of Merit, Royal National Rose Society, 1954.

BELAMI

('Korhanbu') by W. Kordes, 1985. Parentage: ('Prominent' × 'Karina') × 'Emily Post'. Bushy and upright; large corollas of 35 petals, dark, glossy leaves. Fragrant.

BELLE ÉTOILE

by L. Lens, 1971. Parentage: 'Joanna Hill' × 'Tawny Gold'. Corollas not very large, with 30 petals, soft yellow with almost white underside.

BETTER TIMES

by G. H. Hill Co., 1934. Parentage: 'Briarcliff' sport. Very vigorous and compact growth; double corollas, large, dark, coriaceous leaves. Slightly fragrant.

Avon

Aztec

Baccará

Bajazzo

Belle Étoile

Beauté

Belami

Better Times

Bettina

Bingo

Big Dream

Black Lady

Bimboro

Black Tea

Blue Moon

Blue Parfum

BETTINA
('Mepal') by F. Meilland, 1953. Parentage: 'Peace' × ('Mme. Joseph Perraud' × 'Demain'). Well-formed corollas of 37 petals, large, dark, glossy, bronzy leaves. Fragrant.

BIG DREAM
by Jackson & Perkins, 1984. Large corollas of 17–18 petals, fuchsia.

BIMBORO
by Kordes, 1978. Parentage: seedling × 'Kardinal'. Upright and bushy; medium corollas of 46 petals, globular buds, glossy leaves. Fragrant.

BINGO
('Dyna') by Robichon, 1955. Parentage: ('Hadley' seedling × 'Amy Quinard') × 'Crimson Glory'. Upright; very double corollas of 55 petals, large, pointed buds, glossy leaves. Very fragrant.

BLACK LADY
('Taanblady') by Tantau, 1976. Bushy; double corollas, red fading into black, medium size, opaque leaves. Very fragrant.

BLACK TEA
by K. Okamoto, 1973. Parentage: 'Hawaii' × ('Aztec' × ('Goldilocks' × 'Fashion')). Medium height, bushy, with hooked prickles; deep brown corollas of 32 petals, urn-shaped, dark, semiglossy leaves. Slightly fragrant.

BLUE MOON
('Tannacht', 'Mainzer Fastnacht', 'Sissi', 'Blue Monday') by M. Tantau, 1964. Parentage: 'Sterling Silver' seedling × seedling. Vigorous; large corollas of 40 petals, tapered buds. Very fragrant. Gold Medal, Rome, 1964.

BLUE PARFUM
('Tanfifum') by Tantau, 1978. Bushy; large, double corollas, glossy leaves. Very fragrant.

Blue River

Brandy

Bob Hope

Bon Accord

BLUE RIVER
('Korsicht') by W. Kordes, 1984. Parentage: 'Blue Moon' × 'Zorina'. Large corollas of 35 petals, lilac, shaded deeper at edges, medium green, semiglossy leaves. Very fragrant.

BOB HOPE
by R. Kordes, 1966. Parentage: 'Friedrich Schwarz' × 'Kordes' Perfecta'. Tall and vigorous; corollas of 38 petals, very large, dark, coriaceous leaves. Very fragrant.

BON ACCORD
by Anderson's Rose Nursery, 1967. Parentage: 'Prima Ballerina' × 'Percy Thrower'. Corollas pink shaded silver, large, glossy leaves. Fragrant.

BONSOIR
('Dicbo') by A. Dickson, 1968. Full and large corollas, ovoid buds, glossy leaves. Very fragrant. Certificate of Merit, Royal National Rose Society, 1966.

BRANDY
('Arocad') by H. Swim & J. Christensen, 1981. Parentage: 'First Prize' × 'Dr. A. J. Verhage'. Vigorous, medium growth; corollas of 28 petals, intense apricot, mainly solitary, long, tapered buds, large leaves, straight prickles. Slight tea fragrance. All-America Rose Selections Award, 1982.

Bonsoir

BRIDAL ROBE
by McGredy, 1955. Parentage: 'McGredy's Pink' × 'Mrs. Charles Lamplough'. Vigorous; large corollas of 54 petals, olive-green, glossy leaves. Fragrant. Gold Medal, Royal National Rose Society, 1953.

BURGUND '81
('Loving Memory', 'Korgund 81', 'Red Cedar') by W. Kordes, 1981. Parentage: seedling × 'Red Planet' seedling. Upright, bushy; large, double corollas of more than 40 petals, medium green, semiglossy leaves. Slightly fragrant.

CAESAR
('Varbole', 'Carambole') by J. van Veen, 1981. Parentage: 'Ilona' × seedling. Upright, branched growth; globular blooms of 33 petals, ovoid buds, medium green, semiglossy leaves, red prickles. Slight tea fragrance.

CAMELOT
by Swim & Weeks, 1964. Parentage: 'Circus' × 'Queen Elizabeth'. Tall and vigorous; corollas of 48 petals, cupped, large, dark, glossy leaves. Spicy fragrance. All-America Rose Selections Award, 1965.

CANARY
('Tancary') by Tantau, 1972. Corollas double, yellow petals marked orange, medium size. Fragrant.

CANASTA
by Gaujard, 1976. Parentage: 'Karl Herbst' × 'Miss Universe'. Large corollas, fuchsia.

CANDIA
by M. L. Meilland, 1978. Parentage: 'Esther Ofarim' × ('Super Star' × 'Flirt'). Well-formed corollas, white flushed with soft yellow shading into pink on the edges.

CANDY STRIPE
by McCummings, 1963. Parentage: 'Pink Peace' sport. Corollas dusty pink streaked lighter.

Bridal Robe

Burgund '81

Caesar

Camelot

Candia

Canary

Canasta

Candy Stripe

Caprice de Meilland

Cara Mia

Carina

CAPRICE DE MEILLAND
('Lady Eve Price', 'Caprice') by F. Meilland, 1948.
Parentage: 'Peace' × 'Fantastique'. Upright and bushy;
corollas of 24 petals, large, deep pink with reverse cream,
ovoid buds, dark, coriaceous leaves. Slightly fragrant.

CARA MIA
('Dearest One', 'Maja Mauser', 'Natacha', 'Danina') by
G. K. McDaniel, 1969. Upright and vigorous; double
corollas, ovoid buds, glossy leaves. Fragrant.

CARINA
('Meichim') by Alain Meilland, 1963. Parentage: 'White
Knight' × ('Happiness' × 'Independence'). Bushy and
upright; large corollas of 40 petals, coriaceous leaves.
Fragrant.

CARINELLA
by Meilland, 1973. Parentage: 'Carina' sport. Soft pink
corollas. Slightly fragrant.

CARNIVAL
by Archer, 1939. Large corollas of 25 petals.

CARROUSEL
by Duehersen, 1950. Parentage: seedling × 'Margy'.
Upright, vigorous and compact; medium-size corollas of 20
petals, dark, glossy, coriaceous leaves. Fragrant. Gold Medal,
American Rose Society, 1956.

CARTE BLANCHE
('Meiringa') by Paolino, 1975. Parentage: ('Carina' ×
'White Knight') × 'Jack Frost'. Vigorous; large corollas of
38 petals, opaque leaves.

Carinella

Carrousel

Carnival

Carte Blanche

CARTE D'OR
('Supra', 'Meirobidor') by M. L. Meilland, 1980.
Parentage: (('Zambra' × ('Baccará' × 'White Knight'))
× 'Golden Garnette') × seedling. Upright variety, for its
cut flowers; large corollas of 20 petals, dark, semiglossy
leaves. No fragrance.

CATHERINE DENEUVE
('Meipraserpi') by Meilland, 1982. Upright, thick foliage;
double corollas, vermilion shaded orange. Gold Medal Rome,
1979.

CATHRINE KORDES
by Kordes, 1930. Parentage: ('Mme. Caroline Testout' ×
'Willomere') by 'Sensation'. Very large corollas, dark red
buds.

CHAMPAGNER
('Korampa', 'Antique Silk') by Kordes, 1982. Parentage:
'Annabella' seedling × seedling. Upright, compact; large
corollas of 20 petals, medium green, semiglossy leaves.
Slightly fragrant.

CHAMPION
by G. Fryer, 1976. Parentage: 'Irish Gold' × 'Whisky
Mac'. Very large, very double corollas of 50–55 petals,
cream, flushed red and pink, large leaves, light green.
Fragrant.

CHANTILLY LACE
by P. Devor, 1978. Parentage: 'Blue Moon' × 'Angel
Face'. Greenhouse variety; corollas of 35 petals, large, glossy
leaves. Very fragrant.

CHARLES DE GAULLE
('Meilanein', 'Katherine Mansfield') by M. L. Meilland,
1974. Parentage: ('Sissi' × 'Prélude') × ('Kordes'
Sondermeldung' × 'Caprice'). Vigorous; corollas double,
large, globular, then cupped, with 38 petals. Very fragrant.

CHARLES MALLERIN
by F. Meilland, 1951. Parentage: ('Rome Glory' ×
'Congo') × 'Tassin'. Vigorous, irregular growth; flat, large
corollas of 38 petals, blackish crimson, coriaceous, dark
leaves. Very fragrant.

Carte d'Or

Catherine Deneuve

Cathrine Kordes

Chantilly Lace

Champagner

Charles de Gaulle

Champion

Charles Mallerin

Charlotte Armstrong

Chicago Peace

Chiyo

Christian Dior

CHARLOTTE ARMSTRONG
by Lammerts, 1940. Parentage: 'Soeur Thérèse' × 'Crimson Glory'. Vigorous and compact; large corollas of 35 petals.

CHICAGO PEACE
by Johnston, 1962. Parentage: 'Peace' sport. Corollas pink, base canary-yellow. Gold Medal Portland, 1961.

CHIYO
by K. Ota, 1975. Parentage: 'Karl Herbst' × 'Chrysler Imperial'. Vigorous, upright; large corollas of 25 petals, glossy, medium green leaves. Slight fruit fragrance.

CHRISTIAN DIOR
('Meilie') by F. Meilland, 1958. Parentage: ('Independence' × 'Happiness') × ('Peace' × 'Happiness'). Upright, bushy; corollas of 55 petals.

CHRYSLER IMPERIAL
by Lammerts, 1952. Parentage: 'Charlotte Armstrong' × 'Mirandy'. Vigorous, compact; large corollas of 55 petals, pointed buds, dark leaves. Very fragrant. Gold Medal Portland, 1951, All-America Rose Selections, 1953; American Rose Society award, 1964, and Rose Fragrance Medal, 1965.

Chrysler Imperial

City of Bath

Cocktail '80

Claire France

Colorama

Columbus Queen

Comtesse Vandal

Confidence

CITY OF BATH
by Sanday, 1969. Parentage: 'Gavotte' × 'Buccaneer'. Corollas of 55 petals, large, candy pink, reverse lighter, opaque leaves. Fragrant.

CLAIRE FRANCE
by Mondial Roses, 1964. Corollas of 40 petals, double, soft pink.

COCKTAIL '80
by Meilland, 1979. Rounded corollas of 25–30 petals, soft yellow flushed pink. Fragrant.

COLORAMA
('Meirigalu', 'Dr. R. Maag') by M. L. Meilland, 1968. Parentage: 'Suspense' × 'Confidence'. Upright, vigorous and bushy; corollas double, cupped, large, ovoid buds, very glossy leaves. Fragrant.

COLUMBUS QUEEN
by D. L. Armstrong and Swim, 1968. Parentage: 'La Jolla' × seedling. Upright, vigorous; corollas medium of 27 petals, high-centered to cupped, ovoid and pointed buds, dark, coriaceous leaves. Slightly fragrant. Gold Medal Geneva, 1961.

COMTESSE VANDAL
('Countess Vandal') by M. Leenders, 1932. Parentage: ('Ophelia' × 'Mrs. Aron Vard') × 'Souvenir de Claudius Pernet'. Bushy and compact; large corollas of 30 petals, salmon-pink, reverse coppery pink, dark leaves. Fragrant. Gold Medal Bagatelle, 1931.

CONFIDENCE
by F. Meilland, 1951. Parentage: 'Peace' × 'Michèle Meilland'. Upright and bushy; large corollas of 34 petals, ovoid buds, dark, coriaceous leaves. Fragrant. Gold Medal Bagatelle, 1951.

COPPELIA
by F. Meilland, 1952. Parentage: 'Peace' × 'Europa'.
Corollas of 28 petals, yellow changing into scarlet-red.

COQUETTE
by Warriner, 1976. Parentage unknown. Upright; large
corollas of 33 petals, tapered buds, light green leaves with
reverse purple. Slightly fragrant.

CRIMSON GLORY
by Kordes, 1935. Parentage: 'Cathrine Kordes' seedling ×
'W. E. Chaplin'. Vigorous, bushy, with tendency for
spreading growth; corollas large, cupped, of 30 petals,
tapered buds. Strong damascena fragrance. Gold Medal
Royal National Rose Society, 1963, and Rose Fragrance
Medal, 1961.

DAIMONJI
by T. Shibata, 1981. Parentage: seedling × ('Miss Ireland'
× 'Polynesian Sunset'). Bushy, medium height; large
corollas of 48 petals, dark leaves. Slightly fragrant.

DAINTY BESS
by W. E. B. Archer, 1925. Parentage: 'Ophelia' × 'K. of
K.'. Vigorous; corollas single, with five fringed petals, pink
with maroon stamens, coriaceous leaves. Fragrant. Gold
Medal Royal National Rose Society, 1925.

DESERT DREAM
by McGredy, 1955. Parentage: 'R. M. S. Queen Mary' ×
'Mrs. Sam McGredy'. Corollas large, well-formed, light
pink.

DIAMOND JUBILEE
by Boerner, 1947. Parentage: 'Maréchal Niel' × 'Feu
Pernet Ducher'. Upright and compact; large corollas of 28
petals, cupped, ovoid buds, coriaceous leaves. Fragrant. Gold
Medal All-America Rose Selections, 1948.

DIANA
by Tantau, 1977. Medium-large corollas of 30 petals,
intense yellow.

Coppelia

Coquette

Crimson Glory

Daimonji

Diamond Jubilee

Dainty Bess

Diana

Desert Dream

Diorama

Doris Tysterman

Dolce Vita

DIORAMA
by G. de Ruiter, 1965. Parentage: 'Peace' × 'Beauté'. Vigorous, upright; large corollas. Fragrant.

DOLCE VITA
('Deldal') by Delbard, 1971. Parentage: 'Voeux de Bonheur' × ('Chic Parisien' × ('Michèle Meilland' × 'Mme. Joseph Perraud')). Vigorous, upright, and bushy; large corollas of 37 petals. Slightly fragrant.

DORIS TYSTERMAN
by Wisbech Plant Co., 1975. Parentage: 'Peer Gynt' × seedling. Upright; large corollas of 28 petals, tangerine and gold, glossy leaves. Slightly fragrant.

DOUBLE DELIGHT
('Andeli') by Swim & Ellis, 1977. Parentage: 'Granada' × 'Garden Party'. Upright, bushy, with spreading growth; large corollas of 40 petals, creamy white becoming strawberry-red, urn-shaped buds. Spicy fragrance. Gold Medal Baden Baden and Rome, 1976, All-America Rose Selections, 1977, Rose Fragrance Medal, 1986.

Double Delight

DR. DEBAT
('Dr. F. Debat', 'La Rosée') by F. Meilland, 1952.
Parentage: 'Peace' × 'Mrs. John Laing'. Upright, vigorous;
large corollas of 28 petals, coriaceous leaves. Fragrant. Gold
Medal Royal National Rose Society, 1950.

DUET
by Swim, 1960. Parentage: 'Fandango' × 'Roundelay'.
Upright and vigorous; large corollas of 30 petals, light pink
with underside dark pink, coriaceous leaves. Slightly
fragrant. Gold Medal Baden Baden, 1959, and
All-America Rose Selections, 1961.

DUFTGOLD
('Tandugoft', 'Fragrant Gold') by M. Tantau, 1981.
Upright; large, semidouble corollas, dark, glossy leaves.
Fragrant.

DUFTWOLKE
('Fragrant Cloud', 'Tanellis', 'Nuage Parfumé') by M.
Tantau, 1963. Parentage: seedling × 'Prima Ballerina'.
Vigorous, upright; large, well-formed corollas of 28 petals,
coral-red becoming geranium-red, ovoid buds, dark, glossy
leaves. Very fragrant. Gold Medal Portland and Royal
National Rose Society, 1967, and Rose Fragrance Medal,
1969.

DUFTZAUBER
('Kordu', 'Fragrant Charm') by R. Kordes, 1969.
Parentage: 'Prima Ballerina' × 'Kaiserin Farah'. Upright,
medium growth; large, double corollas, ovoid buds, clear
leaves. Very fragrant.

DUFTZAUBER '84
('Korzaun') by W. Kordes, 1984. Parentage: 'Feuerzauber'
× seedling. Upright and bushy; large corollas of 35 petals,
large, dark, semiglossy leaves. Fragrant.

ECLIPSE
by Nicolas, 1935. Parentage: 'Joanna Hill' × 'Federico
Casas'. Vigorous, bushy; corollas of 28 petals, tapered buds,
dark, coriaceous leaves. Fragrant. First bloomed on Eclipse
Day, August 31, 1932. Gold Medal Portland and Rome,
1935, Bagatelle, 1936, American Rose Society, 1938.

Dr. Debat

Duet

Duftgold

Duftwolke

Duftzauber '84

Duftzauber

Eclipse

EDEN ROSE
by F. Meilland, 1950. Parentage: 'Peace' × 'Signora'.
Vigorous and upright; large corollas of 58 petals, cupped,
glossy, bright, dark green leaves. Very fragrant. Gold Medal
Royal National Rose Society, 1950.

EDITOR MCFARLAND
by C. Mallerin, 1931. Parentage: 'Pharisaer' × 'Lallita'.
Vigorous and bushy; large corollas of 30 petals, glowing
pink flushed with yellow. Very fragrant.

EIFFEL TOWER
by D. L. Armstrong and Swim, 1973. Parentage: 'First
Love' × seedling. Upright; large corollas of 35 petals,
tapered buds, urn-shaped, coriaceous, semiglossy leaves. Very
fragrant. Gold Medal Geneva and Rome, 1963.

EIKO
by Suzuki, 1978. Parentage: ('Peace' × 'Charleston') ×
'Kagayaki'. Vigorous; large corollas of 35 petals, yellow and
scarlet, pointed buds, large, glossy, light green leaves. Slightly
fragrant.

ELMARA
by De Ruiter, 1977.

EMBLEM
by Warriner, 1981. Parentage: seedling × 'Sunshine'.
Upright; corollas of 25 petals, dark, glossy leaves, straight,
long, light green prickles. Slightly fragrant.

ENA HARKNESS
by Norman, 1946. Parentage: 'Crimson Glory' ×
'Southport'. Upright; large, double corollas, coriaceous leaves.
Very fragrant. Gold Medal Royal National Rose Society,
1945, and Portland, 1955.

Eden Rose

Editor McFarland

Eiffel Tower

Elmara

Emblem

Eiko

Ena Harkness

Erotika

Espoir

Esmeralda

Ethel Sanday

EROTIKA
('Eroica') by M. Tantau, 1968. Upright; large, well-formed corollas of 33 petals, ovoid buds, dark, glossy leaves. Very fragrant.

ESMERALDA
('Keepsake', 'Kormalda') by Kordes' Söhne, 1981. Bushy; corollas of 40 petals, dark pink blended with light pink shades, retroflexed, ovoid buds, large, dark leaves, thick prickles. Moderately fragrant.

ESPOIR
by Meilland, 1981. Corollas of 35 petals, deep red.

ETHEL JAMES
by S. McGredy, 1921. Large, single corollas, salmon-pink with center flushed yellow.

ETHEL SANDAY
by Mee, 1954. Parentage: 'Rex Anderson' × 'Audrey Cobden'. Upright; large, well-formed corollas of 34 petals, yellow flushed with apricot, dark leaves. Slightly fragrant. Gold Medal Royal National Rose Society, 1953.

Ethel James

Excitement

Fernand Arles

Fan Fare

Fiord

Fiorella

First Federal's Renaissance

First Love

EXCITEMENT
*by Robert Jelly, 1985. Parentage: 'Golden Fantasie' ×
'Coed'. Well-formed corollas of 20 petals, deep yellow.*

FAN FARE
*by Roy L. Byrum, 1981. Parentage: 'Cotillon' × 'Hosier
Gold'. Vigorous; corollas of 23 petals, short, pointed buds,
short, straight, broad-based prickles. Slightly fragrant.*

FERNAND ARLES
*by Gaujard, 1949. Parentage: 'Mme. Joseph Perraud' ×
seedling. Large corollas, salmon flushed soft red. Fruit
fragrance.*

FIORD
*by Meilland, 1986. Well-formed corollas of 30–35 petals,
red flushed cyclamen-pink.*

FIORELLA
*by Meilland, 1980. Parentage: 'Sonia' sport. Medium
corollas of 25 petals, deep pink.*

FIRST FEDERAL'S RENAISSANCE
*by Warriner, 1980. Parentage: seedling × 'First Prize'.
Compact; large corollas of 23 petals, medium pink flushed
light pink, long and pointed buds, large leaves. Slightly
fragrant.*

FIRST LOVE
*('Premier Amour') by Swim, 1951. Parentage: 'Charlotte
Armstrong' × 'Show Girl'. Moderately bushy; medium
corollas of 25 petals, tapered and pointed buds, coriaceous,
light green leaves. Slightly fragrant.*

FIRST PRIZE

*by Boerner, 1970. Parentage: 'Enchantment' seedling ×
'Golden Masterpiece' seedling. Vigorous and upright; very
large, double corollas, pink, with center flushed ivory, tapered
and pointed buds, coriaceous, dark leaves. Fragrant.
All-America Rose Selections Award, 1970, and American
Rose Society, 1971.*

FRIENDSHIP

*('Linrick') by Lindquist, 1978. Parentage: 'Fragrant
Cloud' × 'Miss All-American Beauty'. Vigorous and
upright; large corollas of 28 petals, cupped to flat, dark
leaves. Very fragrant. All-America Rose Selections Award,
1979.*

FRITZ THIEDEMANN

*by M. Tantau, 1959. Parentage: 'Horstmann's
Jubiläeumrose' × 'Circus'. Bushy; well-formed, large
corollas of 36 petals, dark leaves. Fragrant.*

FROHSINN '82

*('Tansinnroh') by M. Tantau, 1982. Large corollas of 35
petals, apricot and peach shadings, large, glossy, dark leaves.
Slightly fragrant.*

FUSHIMI

*by Keihan Hirakata, 1986. Well-formed corollas of 40
petals, deep pink with lighter underside. Slightly fragrant.*

GALLIVARDA

*by Kordes' Söhne, 1977. Parentage: 'Colour Wonder' ×
'Wiener Charme'. Upright; large corollas of 34 petals, red
with yellow underside, tapered and pointed buds, glossy
leaves. Slightly fragrant.*

GARDEN PARTY

*by H. Swim, 1959. Parentage: 'Charlotte Armstrong' ×
'Peace'. Bushy, well-branched growth; large corollas of 28
petals, high-centered to cupped, pale yellow to white, flushed
with light pink, urn-shaped buds, semiglossy leaves. Slightly
fragrant. Gold Medal Bagatelle, 1959, All-America Rose
Selections, 1960.*

GOLD MEDAL

*('Aroyquel') by J. Christensen, 1982. Parentage: 'Yellow
Pages' × ('Grenada' × 'Garden Party'). Vigorous and
disease resistant; corollas deep yellow, abundant, medium
green, opaque leaves. Also classified among the Grandiflora.*

First Prize

Friendship

Fritz Thiedemann

Frohsinn '82

Gallivarda

Garden Party

Fushimi

Gold Medal

Ginger Rogers

Golden Giant

Gilbert Bécaud

Golden Masterpiece

Golden Emblem

Golden Medaillon

Golden Rapture

Golden Scepter

Goldene Sonne

GINGER ROGERS
('Salmon Charm') by S. McGredy, 1969. Parentage: 'Tropicana' × 'Miss Ireland'. Very tall; large corollas of 30 petals, light green leaves. Fragrant.

GILBERT BÉCAUD
('Meiridorio') by M. L. Meilland, 1979. Parentage: ('Peace' × 'Mrs. John Laing') × 'Bettina'. Upright; large corollas of 45 petals, yellow and orange shadings, bronze, opaque leaves. Slightly fragrant.

GOLDEN EMBLEM
('Jacgold') by Warriner, 1982. Parentage: ('Bridal Pink' × 'Dr. A. J. Verhage') × ('Golden Sun' × 'South Seas'). Upright; large corollas of 20 petals, medium green, glossy leaves. Slightly fragrant.

GOLDEN GIANT
('Fièvre d'Or', 'Goldraush') by R. Kordes, 1961. Vigorous and tall; well-formed, large corollas of 45 petals, dark leaves. Fragrant. Gold Medal Royal National Rose Society, 1960.

GOLDEN MASTERPIECE
by Boerner, 1954. Parentage: 'Mandalay' × 'Golden Scepter'. Upright; very large corollas of 35 petals, tapered and pointed buds, very glossy leaves. Fragrant.

GOLDEN MEDAILLON
('Limelight', 'Korikon') by W. Kordes, 1984. Parentage: 'Peach Melba' × seedling. Upright, bushy, with tendency for spreading growth; large corollas of 35 petals, dark, semiglossy leaves. Very fragrant.

GOLDEN RAPTURE
('Geheimrat Duisberg') by Kordes, 1933. Parentage: 'Rapture' × 'Julien Potin'. Vigorous; very large corollas of 40 petals, pointed buds, glossy leaves. Fragrant.

GOLDEN SCEPTER
('Spek's Yellow') by Verschuren-Pechtold, 1950. Parentage: 'Golden Rapture' × seedling. Vigorous and upright; large corollas of 35 petals, pointed buds, coriaceous, glossy leaves. Fragrant.

GOLDEN SONNE
('Golden Sun') by R. Kordes, 1957. Parentage: ('Walter Bentley' × 'Condesa de Sástago') × 'Golden Scepter'. Upright and bushy; large, double, whirling corollas, glossy leaves. Fragrant.

Goldkrone

Gordon Eddie

Grace de Monaco

GOLDKRONE
('Gold Crown', 'Corona de Oro', 'Couronne d'Or') by R. Kordes, 1960. Parentage: 'Peace' × 'Golden Scepter'. Vigorous, upright; large, well-formed corollas of 35 petals, dark, coriaceous leaves. Fragrant.

GORDON EDDIE
by Eddie, 1949. Parentage: 'Royal Visit' × 'Cynthia Brooke'. Large, beautifully shaped corollas of 40 petals, soft apricot.

GRACE DE MONACO
('Meimit') by F. Meilland, 1956. Parentage: 'Peace' × 'Michèle Meiklland'. Vigorous, bushy; large, double, well-formed corollas, coriaceous leaves. Very fragrant.

GRANADA
('Donatella') by Lindquist, 1963. Parentage: 'Tiffany' × 'Cavalcade'. Vigorous and upright; large corollas of 23 petals, blend of pink-orange-yellow lemon, urn-shaped buds, coriaceous, crinkled leaves. Fragrant. All-America Rose Selections award, 1964, Rose Fragrance Medal, 1968.

GRANDE DUCHESSE CHARLOTTE
by Ketten Bros., 1942. Vigorous, bushy; large corollas of 25 petals, dark, glossy leaves. Slightly fragrant. Gold Medal Rome, 1938, Portland, 1941, All-America Rose Selections, 1943.

GRAND MASTERPIECE
by Warriner, 1978. Parentage: seedling × 'Tonight'. Large, well-formed corollas, velvet red.

GRAND'MÈRE JENNY
by F. Meilland, 1950. Parentage: 'Peace' × ('Julien Potin' × 'Sensation'). Vigorous; large corollas of 30 petals, apricot flushed and edged pink, dark, glossy leaves. Fragrant. Gold Medal Royal National Rose Society, 1950, and Rome, 1955.

GRANDPA DICKSON
('Irish Gold') by A. Dickson, 1966. Parentage: ('Kordes' Perfecta' × 'Governador Braga da Cruz') × 'Piccadilly'. Vigorous, upright, and bushy; very large corollas of 33 petals, ovoid buds, dark, glossy, coriaceous leaves. Fragrant. Gold Medal Royal National Rose Society, 1965, The Hague, 1966, and Belfast, 1968.

Granada

Grande Duchesse Charlotte

Grand'mère Jenny

Grand Masterpiece

Grandpa Dickson

Grisbi

Grüss an Berlin

Grüss an Teplitz

Halloween

Hanaguruma

Hanayome

Happiness

Harmonie

GRISBI

('Sunlight') by F. Meilland, 1956. Parentage: ('Eclipse' × 'Ophelia') × 'Montecarlo'. Vigorous, bushy; large corollas of 45 petals, turbinate to cupped, ovoid buds, coriaceous leaves. Fragrant.

GRÜSS AN BERLIN

('Greetings') by R. Kordes, 1963. Vigorous, upright, and bushy; large corollas of 40 petals, dark, glossy leaves. Slightly fragrant.

GRÜSS AN TEPLITZ

('Virginia R. Coxe') by Geschwind, 1897. Parentage: (('Sir Joseph Paxton' × 'Fellenberg') × 'Papa Gontier') × 'Gloire des Rosomanes'. Vigorous and bushy, suitable for hedges; corollas of 33 petals, small, ovoid buds, dark leaves tinted bronze during young growth. Strong spicy fragrance. Also classified among the Bourbons.

HALLOWEEN

by A. P. Howard, 1962. Parentage: ('Peace' × 'Fred Howard') × seedling. Vigorous, upright; large corollas of 65 petals, dark, glossy, coriaceous leaves. Very fragrant.

HANAGURUMA

by K. Teranishi, 1977. Parentage: 'Kordes' Perfecta' × ('Kordes' Perfecta' × 'American Heritage'). Upright; very large corollas of 55 petals, globular buds, light green leaves. Slightly fragrant.

HANAYOME

by Keihan Hirakata, 1970. Parentage: 'Michèle Meilland' × 'Ann Letts'. Corollas of 40 petals, soft pink flushed white. Slightly fragrant.

HAPPINESS

('Rouge Meilland') by F. Meilland, 1949. Parentage: ('Rome Glory' × 'Tassin') × ('Charles P. Kilham' × 'Capucine Chambard'). Vigorous and upright; large corollas of 38 petals. Slightly fragrant.

HARMONIE

('Kortember') by W. Kordes, 1981. Parentage: 'Fragrant Cloud' × 'Uwe Seeler'. Vigorous, upright, and bushy; corollas of 20 petals, salmon-pink with yellow underside, semiglossy leaves. Slightly fragrant. Gold Medal Baden Baden, 1981.

HAWAII
by Boerner, 1960. Parentage: 'Golden Masterpiece' × seedling. Vigorous, upright; large corollas of 33 petals, coriaceous leaves. Very fragrant.

HEIAN
by Keihan Hirakata, 1979. Parentage: 'Hawaii' × ('Aztec' × 'Fashion'). Corollas of 40 petals, vermilion.

HELENE SCHOEN
by Von Abrams, 1963. Parentage: 'Multnomah' × 'Charles Mallerin'. Vigorous and upright; very double corollas of 60 petals, large, tapered, and pointed buds, glossy, coriaceous leaves. Slightly fragrant.

HELEN TRAUBEL
by Swim, 1951. Parentage: 'Charlotte Armstrong' × 'Glowing Sunset'. Tall and vigorous; large, flat corollas of 23 petals set on weak steles, pink to apricot, tapered and pointed buds, glossy, coriaceous leaves. Fragrant. Gold Medal Rome, 1951, All-America Rose Selections, 1952.

HELMUT SCHMIDT
('Korbelma', 'Simba', 'Goldsmith') by W. Kordes, 1979. Parentage: 'New Day' × seedling. Vigorous, upright, and bushy; corollas of 35 petals, large, tapered, and pointed buds, opaque leaves. Fragrant. Gold Medal Belgium and Geneva, 1979.

HENKELL ROYAL
by R. Kordes, 1964. Vigorous, bushy; large, double, well-formed corollas. Very fragrant. Gold Medal Baden Baden, 1964.

HENRY FORD
by A. P. Howard, 1954. Parentage: 'Pink Dawn' climbing × 'The Doctor'. Vigorous, upright; large corollas of 30 petals, silvery pink, tapered buds. Fragrant.

Hawaii

Heian

Helene Schoen

Helen Traubel

Helmut Schmidt

Henkell Royal

Henry Ford

High Esteem

Hohoemi

Hoh-Jun

Hi-Ohgi

HIDALGO
('Meitulandi') by M. L. Meilland, 1979. Parentage:
(('Queen Elizabeth' × 'Karl Herbst') × ('Lady X' ×
'Pharaoh')) × ('Meicesar' × 'Papa Meilland'). Vigorous,
upright; very large corollas of 30 petals, cupped, opaque
leaves tending toward bronze. Very fragrant.

HIGH ESTEEM
by von Abrams, 1961. Parentage: ('Charlotte Armstrong'
× 'Mme. Henri Guillot') × ('Multnomah' × 'Charles
Mallerin'). Vigorous, upright, and compact; large corollas of
43 petals, pink with silvery underside, pointed buds,
coriaceous, light green leaves. Strong fruity fragrance.

HI-OHGI
by S. Suzuki, 1981. Parentage: 'San Francisco' ×
('Montezume' × 'Peace'). Tall, upright; large corollas of 28
petals, dark, semiglossy leaves, prickles slanted downward.
Fragrant.

HOHOEMI
by S. Suzuki, 1977. Parentage: ('Chrysler Imperial' ×
'Dorothy Goodwin') × 'Percy Thrower'.

HOH-JUN
by S. Suzuki, 1981. Parentage: 'Granada' × 'Flaming
Peace'. Compact growth; corollas of 28 petals, cup-shaped,
pink suffused red, dark, semiglossy leaves, large prickles.

Hidalgo

Hoku-to

Ikaruga

Honey Favorite

Inka

Honor

Interflora

Intermezzo

Irish Fireflame

Isabel de Ortiz

HOKU-TO
by S. Suzuki, 1979. Parentage: ('Myoo-Jo' × 'Chicago Peace') × 'King's Ransom'. Vigorous, upright, with tendency toward spreading growth; corollas of 42 petals, light green, large leaves. Fragrant.

HONEY FAVORITE
by Von Abrams, 1962. Parentage: 'Pink Favorite' sport. Corollas pale rose on yellow base.

HONOR
('Jacolite', 'Michèle Torr') by Warriner, 1980. Upright; large, open corollas of 23 petals, large, dark leaves. Slightly fragrant. All-America Rose Selections award, 1980.

IKARUGA
by R. Ito, 1975. Parentage: 'McGredy's Ivory' × 'Garden Party'. Large corollas of 30 petals, white flushed yellow. Slightly fragrant.

INKA
('Tantreika') by Tantau, 1978. Upright, bushy; large, double corollas of 30–35 petals, deep pink, glossy leaves.

INTERFLORA
('Interview') by Meilland, 1968. Parentage: (('Baccará' × 'White Knight') × ('Baccará' × 'Jolie Madame')) × ('Baccará' × 'Paris Match'). Greenhouse variety, vigorous, upright; large corollas of 40 petals, coriaceous leaves. Slightly fragrant.

INTERMEZZO
by S. Dot, 1963. Parentage: 'Grey Pearl' × 'Lila Vidri'. Moderately tall, compact; medium corollas of 25 petals, ovoid buds, dark, glossy leaves. Fragrant.

IRISH FIREFLAME
by A. Dickson, 1914. Bushy, compact growth; large, single corollas of 5 petals, orange to gold veined crimson, dark, glossy leaves. Very fragrant. Gold Medal Royal National Rose Society, 1912.

ISABEL DE ORTIZ
('Isabel Ortiz') by R. Kordes, 1965. Parentage: 'Peace' × 'Kordes' Perfecta'. Vigorous, upright; large, well-formed corollas of 38 petals, pink with silvery underside, dark, glossy leaves. Fragrant. Gold Medal Madrid, 1960, and Royal National Rose Society, 1961.

IWASHIMIZU
by T. Tanaka, 1969. Parentage: 'Garden Party' × 'Izayoi'.

IZAYOI
by T. Tanaka, 1968. Parentage: 'McGredy's Ivory' × 'Lunelle'. Corollas of 35 petals, white flushed soft yellow.

JANINA
by Tantau, 1974. Small, well-formed corollas, intense orange flushed yellow. Fragrant.

JARDINS DE BAGATELLE
by Meilland, 1985. Corollas of 50 petals, soft pink becoming white.

JELRAFLOKI
by Meilland, 1984. Well-formed corollas of 30 petals, vermilion.

JELVANICA
by Meilland, 1980. Parentage: 'Baccará' × seedling.

JOHN F. KENNEDY
by Boerner, 1965. Parentage: seedling × 'White Queen'. Vigorous; large corollas of 48 petals, ovoid buds, coriaceous leaves. Fragrant.

JOHN S. ARMSTRONG
by H. Swim, 1961. Parentage: 'Charlotte Armstrong' × seedling. Tall and bushy; large corollas of 40 petals, turbinate to cupped, coriaceous, semiglossy leaves. Slightly fragrant. Gold Medal All-America Rose Selections, 1962.

Iwashimizu

Izayoi

Janina

Jardins de Bagatelle

Jelvanica

Jelrafloki

John F. Kennedy

John S. Armstrong

Jolie Madame

Josephine Bruce

Julie

JOLIE MADAME
by F. Meilland, 1960. Parentage: ('Independence' × 'Happiness') × 'Better Times'. Vigorous, upright, bushy; large, very double corollas of 65 petals, cupped, coriaceous, glossy leaves. Slightly fragrant.

JOSEPHINE BAKER
('Velvet Flame', 'Meimaur') by Meilland, 1963. Parentage: 'Tropicana' × 'Papa Meilland'. Vigorous; large corollas of 30 petals, dark leaves. Slightly fragrant.

JOSEPHINE BRUCE
by Bees, 1949. Parentage: 'Crimson Glory' × 'Madge Whipp'. Vigorous, branched growth; large corollas of 24 petals, dark leaves. Slightly fragrant.

JULIE
by R. Kordes, 1970. Parentage: seedling × 'Red American Beauty'. Upright; large, double corollas, cupped, ovoid buds, dark, soft leaves. Very fragrant.

JUST JOEY
by Cants of Colchester, 1972. Parentage: 'Fragrant Cloud' × 'Dr. A. J. Verhange'. Moderate growth; large, classic corollas of 30 petals, rippling form, glossy, coriaceous leaves. Very fragrant.

Just Joey

Josephine Baker

Jonetsu

JONETSU
by S. Suzuki, 1978. Parentage: ('Kagayaki' × 'Prima Ballerina') × 'Kagayaki'.

KABUKI
('Meigold', 'Golden Prince') by M. L. Meilland, 1968. Parentage: ('Monte Carlo' × 'Bettina') × ('Peace' × 'Soraya'). Vigorous, upright; medium corollas of 45 petals, bronzy, glossy, coriaceous leaves. Fragrant.

KAGARIBI
by T. Oshima, 1970. Parentage: 'Piccadilly' sport. Corollas of 20–28 petals, scarlet streaked yellow with yellow underside.

Kabuki

Kagaribi

KAGAYAKI
(*'Brilliant Light'*) *by S. Suzuki, 1970. Parentage: (*'Aztec'*
seedling* × (*'Spectacular'* × *'Aztec'*)) × *'Cover Girl'*
seedling. Vigorous, upright; large, double corollas, glossy,
dark leaves. Slightly fragrant.*

KAMO
by Keihan Hirakata, 1978. Parentage: ('Michèle Meilland'*
× *'Ann Letts'*) × *'Hanayome'*. Corollas of 30–40 petals,
soft pink edged deeper pink.*

KAN-PAI
by S. Suzuki, 1980. Parentage: ('Yu-ai'* × (*'Happiness'*
× *'American Beauty'*)) × *'Pharaoh'*. Upright; corollas of
48 petals, dark leaves. Fragrant. Gold Medal Rome, 1983.*

Kamo

Kan-pai

Kagayaki

KARDINAL

('Korlingo') by W. Kordes, 1985. Parentage: seedling ×
'Flamingo'. Upright; large corollas of 35 petals, dark,
semiglossy leaves. Slightly fragrant.

KARL HERBST

('Red Peace') by Kordes, 1950. Parentage: 'Independence'
× 'Peace'. Vigorous; well-formed corollas with large petals.
Very fragrant. Gold Medal Royal National Rose Society,
1950.

KIBOH

by S. Suzuki, 1986. Parentage: 'Liberty Bell' ×
'Kagayaki'. Vigorous and upright; large corollas of 50
petals, cupped, dark, semiglossy leaves, prickles slanted
downward. Slightly fragrant. Gold Medal The Hague,
1985.

KING'S RANSOM

by Morey, 1961. Parentage: 'Golden Masterpiece' ×
'Lydia'. Vigorous and upright; large corollas of 38 petals,
ovoid buds, coriaceous, glossy leaves. Fragrant. All-America
Rose Selections award, 1962.

KINKAKU

by K. Okamoto, 1975. Parentage: seedling × 'Peace'.
Bushy, medium height; large corollas of 38 petals, light
green leaves, chestnut-brown prickles. Slightly fragrant.

KINUGASA

by T. Shibata, 1984. Parentage: 'Michèle Meilland' ×
('Michèle Meilland' × 'Ann Letts'). Medium height,
bushy; large corollas of 45 petals, light green leaves, hooked,
chestnut-brown prickles. Fruity fragrance.

KITANO

by Keihan Hirakata, 1985. Parentage: 'Kinkaku' ×
'Hanayome'. Corollas of 30–45 petals, white flushed soft
yellow.

KLAUS STÖRTEBEKER

by R. Kordes, 1962. Low, bushy growth; well-formed
corollas of 40 petals, large, dark leaves.

KOISAN

by K. Teranishi, 1969. Parentage: 'Reiko' × 'Miss
Ireland'. Large corollas of 35 petals, coral-pink with soft
yellow underside.

Kardinal

Karl Herbst

Kiboh

King's Ransom

Kitano

Kinkaku

Klaus Störtebeker

Kinugasa

Koisan

Kölner Karneval

Konrad Henkel

Königin Beatrix

Königin der Rosen

KÖLNER KARNEVAL
('Blue Girl', 'Cologne Carnival') by R. Kordes, 1964.
Vigorous, bushy; large, well-formed corollas of 40 petals,
silvery lilac-blue, dark leaves.

KÖNIGIN BEATRIX
('Hetkora', 'Queen Beatrix') by W. Kordes, 1983.
Parentage: seedling × 'Patricia'. Upright, bushy; large
corollas of 35 petals, semiglossy, medium green leaves. Very
fragrant.

KÖNIGIN DER ROSEN
('Colour Wonder', 'Queen of Roses', 'Reine des Roses',
'Korbico') by R. Kordes, 1964. Parentage: 'Kordes'
Perfecta' × 'Tropicana'. Vigorous, bushy; large corollas of
50 petals, coral blue with cream white underside, ovoid buds,
glossy, bronzy leaves, large and numerous prickles. Slightly
fragrant. Gold Medal Belfast, 1966.

KONRAD HENKEL
('Korjet') by W. Kordes, 1983. Parentage: seedling × 'Red
Planet'. Upright, bushy; large corollas of 35 petals, medium
green, semiglossy leaves. Fragrant.

KORDES' PERFECTA
('Koralu', 'Perfecta') by Kordes, 1957. Parentage: 'Golden
Scepter' × 'Karl Herbst'. Vigorous, upright; large corollas of
68 petals, dark, coriaceous, glossy leaves. Very fragrant.
Gold Medal Royal National Rose Society, 1957, and
Portland, 1958.

Kordes' Perfecta

Kosai

Kronenbourg

Koto

Kurama

Kuroshinju

La France

Lady Luck

Lady Rose

KOSAI
by S. Suzuki, 1987. Parentage: 'Duftwolke' × 'Kagayaki'. Corollas of 30 to 35 petals, brilliant scarlet with a yellow base.

KOTO
by S. Suzuki, 1972. Parentage: 'Lydia' seedling × 'Peace' seedling. Large, well-formed corollas, yellow. Fruity fragrance.

KRONENBOURG
('Flaming Peace', 'Macbo') by McGredy, 1965. Parentage: 'Peace' sport. Corollas bright red, with straw-yellow underside veined red.

KURAMA
by Keihan Hirakata, 1977. Parentage: 'Isabel de Ortiz' × 'Christian Dior'. Corollas of 40 petals, red with creamy yellow underside.

KUROSHINJU
by S. Suzuki, 1988. Parentage ('Josephine Bruce' × ('Adventure' × 'Maria Callas')) × 'Cara Mia'. Corollas of 20–25 petals, dark red.

LA FRANCE
by Guillot, 1867. Parentage: 'Mme. Victor Verdier' × 'Mme. Bravy'. Vigorous; large corollas of 60 petals, silvery pink with glowing pink underside, tapered buds. Very fragrant.

LADY LUCK
by A. J. Miller, 1956. Parentage: 'Tom Breneman' × 'Show Girl'. Vigorous, upright, bushy; large corollas of 38 petals, tapered buds, dark, coriaceous leaves. Strong damascena fragrance.

LADY ROSE
by Barni, 1987. Moderate growth; corollas of 35 petals, persistent orange, generous blooming. Slightly fragrant.

LADY X

('Meifigu') by M. L. Meilland, 1966. Parentage: seedling × 'Simone'. Vigorous, upright; large, double corollas, tapered and pointed buds, coriaceous leaves. Slightly fragrant.

LAGUNA

by Kordes, 1974. Parentage: 'Hawaii' × 'Orange Delbard'. Vigorous and upright; double, cupped corollas, large, pointed buds, glossy leaves. Fragrant.

LANDORA

('Sunblest') by Tantau, 1970. Parentage: seedling × 'King's Ransom'. Large corollas of 38 petals, glossy leaves. Slightly fragrant. Gold Medal Tokyo, 1971, and New Zealand, 1973.

LAS VEGAS

('Korgane') by W. Kordes, 1981. Parentage: 'Ludwigshafen am Rhein' × 'Feuerzaber'. Upright, vigorous, and bushy; corollas of 26 petals, large and pointed buds, chestnut-brown prickles. Fragrant. Gold Medal Genoa, 1985.

LAURA '81

('Meidragelac') by M. L. Meilland, 1974. Parentage: ('Pharaoh' × 'Colour Wonder') × (('Suspense' × 'Suspense') × 'King's Ransom'). Medium height; large corollas of 30 petals, small, dark, and semiglossy leaves. Slightly fragrant. Gold Medal Tokyo, 1981.

LEMON SPICE

by D. L. Armstrong and Swim, 1966. Parentage: 'Helen Traubel' × seedling. Vigorous, spreading growth; large, double corollas, tapered and pointed buds, dark, coriaceous leaves. Very fragrant.

LIBERTY BELL

('Freiheitsglocke') by R. Kordes, 1963. Large, double corollas, deep pink with silvery underside.

LIDO DI ROMA

('Delgap') by Delbard-Chabert, 1968. Parentage: ('Chic Parisien' × 'Michèle Meilland') × ('Sultane' × 'Mme. Joseph Perraud'). Vigorous, upright, and bushy; large, double corollas, tapered and pointed buds, coriaceous, glossy leaves. Slightly fragrant. Gold Medal Tokyo, 1968.

Lady X

Laguna

Landora

Las Vegas

Laura '81

Lemon Spice

Liberty Bell

Lido di Roma

Lifrane

Love

Lilac Time

Louis de Funès

Lusambo

Lydia

Lustige

Mme. Butterfly

LIFRANE
by Zwemstra, 1976. Parentage: 'Sonia' sport. Corollas of 20–25 petals, soft violet-pink. Fragrant.

LILAC TIME
by McGredy, 1956. Parentage: 'Golden Dawn' × 'Luis Brinas'. Moderate growth; medium corollas of 33 petals, light green leaves. Fragrant.

LOUIS DE FUNES
by Meilland, 1984. Upright, vigorous, tall; very large corollas of 30 petals, glowing yellow suffused tangerine, bright colored leaves. Gold Medal Monza and Geneva, 1983.

LOVE
by Warriner, 1980. Parentage: unknown × 'Redgold'. Corollas of 35 petals, red with white underside.

LUSAMBO
by Meilland, 1973. Parentage: unknown × 'Pharaon'. Corollas of 20–25 petals, scarlet.

LUSTIGE
('Lukor', 'Jolly') by Kordes, 1973. Parentage: 'Peace' × 'Brandenburg'. Vigorous and upright; large, double, cupped corollas, bronze-red with yellow underside, ovoid buds, large, coriaceous, glossy leaves. Fragrant.

LYDIA
by H. Robinson, 1949. Parentage: 'Phyllis Gold' × seedling. Corollas of 25–30 petals, deep yellow with red streaks at a young stage. Fruity fragrance.

MME. BUTTERFLY
by E. G. Hill, 1918. Parentage: 'Ophelia' sport. Corollas of 25–30 petals, light creamy pink.

Mme. Marie Curie

Madelon

Mme. Sachi

Mme. Violet

MME. CHARLES SAUVAGE
('Mississippi') by C. Mallerin, 1949. Parentage: 'Julien Potin' × 'Orange Nassau'. Bushy; large, well-formed corollas of 30 petals, yellow suffused saffron with orange center. Slightly fragrant.

MME. MARIE CURIE
('Québec') by Gaujard, 1943. Bushy, compact; large corollas of 25 petals, dark, coriaceous leaves. Slightly fragrant. All-America Rose Selections award, 1944.

MME. SACHI
by Jelly, 1985. Parentage: 'Bridal Pink' × seedling. Corollas of 8–10 petals, white on a cream base.

MME. VIOLET
by K. Teranishi, 1981. Parentage: (('Lady X' × 'Sterling Silver') × ('Lady X' × 'Sterling Silver')) × the same. Tall and upright; medium corollas of 45 petals, semiglossy leaves. Slightly fragrant.

MADELON
('Ruimeva') by G. de Ruiter, 1981. Parentage: 'Varlon' × 'Meigenon'. Greenhouse variety, upright; medium corollas of 20 petals, semiglossy leaves.

Mme. Charles Sauvage

Magic Moment

Maioogi

MAGIC MOMENT
by Buyl Frères, 1964. Large, well-formed corollas.

MAIOOGI
*by Keihan Hirakata, 1988. Parentage: seed plant ×
'Christian Dior'.*

MAJEURE
*('Tanya') by Combe, 1959. Parentage: 'Peace' × ('Peace'
× 'Orange Nassau').*

MAJORETTE
*by Meilland, 1967. Parentage: 'Zambra' × 'Fred
Edmunds'.*

MANOU MEILLAND
*('Meitulimon') by M. L. Meilland, 1979. Parentage:
('Baronne Edmond de Rothschild' × 'Baronne Edmond de
Rothschild') × ('Ma Fille' × 'Love Song'). Vigorous,
bushy; medium, cupped corollas of 50 petals, conical buds,
dark, glossy leaves. Slightly fragrant.*

Majeure

Majorette

Manou Meilland

Mardi Gras

Maruyama

Margaret McGredy

Maria Callas

Mascotte '77

Massabielle

McGredy's Ivory

Medallion

MARDI GRAS
by G. L. Jordan, 1953. Parentage: 'Crimson Glory' × 'Poinsettia'. Vigorous, upright, bushy; large corollas of 33 petals, ovoid buds, coriaceous leaves. Fragrant. Gold Medal Baden Baden, 1953.

MARGARET MCGREDY
by McGredy, 1927. Parentage unknown. Vigorous; large corollas of 35 petals, light, coriaceous, glossy leaves. Fragrant. Gold Medal Royal National Rose Society, 1925.

MARIA CALLAS
('Miss All-American Beauty', 'Meidaud') by M. L. Meilland, 1965. Parentage: 'Chrysler Imperial' × 'Karl Herbst'. Vigorous, bushy; large, cupped corollas of 55 petals, coriaceous leaves. Very fragrant. All-America Rose Selections award, 1968.

MARUYAMA
by S. Suzuki, 1984. Parentage: ('Montezuma' × 'Super Star') × Königin der Rosen.

MASCOTTE 77
('Meitiloly') by Paolino, 1976. Parentage: (('Meirendal' × ('Rim' × 'Peace')) × 'Peace'. Vigorous; large corollas of 40 petals, yellow edged red, glossy leaves. Slightly fragrant. Gold Medal Belfast, 1979.

MASSABIELLE
by M. Guillot, 1958. Large, well-formed corollas, white.

MCGREDY'S IVORY
('Portadown Ivory') by McGredy, 1928. Parentage: 'Mrs. Charles Lamplough' × 'Mabel Morse'. Vigorous; large corollas of 28 petals, white on a yellow base, long buds, dark, glossy, coriaceous leaves. Rosa damascena fragrance. Gold Medal Royal National Rose Society, 1928.

MEDALLION
by Warriner, 1973. Parentage: 'South Seas' × 'King's Ransom'. Vigorous, upright; very large, double corollas, large, coriaceous leaves. Fragrant. Gold Medal All-America Rose Selections, 1973.

MEGAMI
by S. Suzuki, 1980. Parentage: seedling × 'Duftwolke'.
Corollas of 25–30 petals, coral-pink.

MEIRINLOR
by Paolino, 1975. Parentage: 'Golden Garnette' ×
(('Golden Garnette' × 'Bettina') × 'Dr. A. J. Verhage').
Large, semidouble corollas of 15–18 petals, dark leaves.

MELINA
('Sir Harry Pilkington', 'Tanema') by H. Wheatcroft
Gardening, 1974. Parentage: 'Inge Horstmann' × 'Sophia
Loren'. Large, well-formed corollas of 30 petals, dark leaves.
Slightly fragrant.

MELODY FAIR
Parentage: 'Sonia' sport. Large corollas, pink flushed coral,
glossy, dark leaves.

MEMORIAM
by Von Abrams, 1961. Parentage: ('Blanche Mallerin' ×
'Peace') × ('Peace' × 'Frau Karl Druschki'). Moderate
growth; large corollas of 55 petals, pastel pink to white,
dark, coriaceous leaves. Fragrant. Gold Medal Portland,
1960.

MESSAGE
('White Knight', 'Meban') by F. Meilland, 1955.
Parentage: ('Virgo' × 'Peace') × 'Virgo'. Vigorous,
upright; large corollas of 33 petals, tapered and pointed buds,
light green, coriaceous leaves. All-America Rose Selections
award, 1958.

MIKADO
By Suzuki, 1987. Parentage: 'Duftwolke' × 'Kagayaki'.
Deep coral-red, glossy leaves. All-America Rose Selections
award, 1988.

MICHÈLE MEILLAND
by F. Meilland, 1945. Parentage: 'Joanna Hill' × 'Peace'.
Vigorous; large, double corollas, light pink shaded lilac with
salmon center.

MILDRED SCHEEL
('Deep Secret') by Tantau, 1977. Vigorous and upright;
large corollas of 40 petals, glossy, dark leaves. Very fragrant.

Megami

Meirinlor

Melina

Melody Fair

Mikado

Memoriam

Michèle Meilland

Message

Mildred Scheel

Milord

Miss Canada

Miriana

Miss France

Miss Blanche

Miss Ireland

MILORD
*by McGredy, 1962. Parentage: 'Rubayat' × 'Karl Herbst'.
Vigorous, upright; globular, double corollas, semiglossy leaves
bronzy in youth. Slightly fragrant. Certificate of Merit
Royal National Rose Society, 1962.*

MIRIANA
*('Meiburgana') by M. L. Meilland, 1981. Parentage:
((seedling × 'Independence') × 'Suspense') × (('Alain' ×
Rosa mutabilis) × 'Caprice') × 'Pharaoh'). Upright;
large corollas with 40 and more petals, semiglossy leaves. No
fragrance.*

MISS BLANCHE
*('Kojack') by Warriner, 1980. Parentage: 'Evening Star' ×
'Coquette'. Upright; corollas of 38 petals, urn-shaped,
tapered buds, large, coriaceous leaves, upright, reddish
prickles. Slightly fragrant.*

MISS CANADA
*by Blakeney, 1963. Parentage: 'Peace' × 'Karl Herbst'.
Vigorous, spreading growth; double corollas, magenta-pink
with silver underside, glossy, coriaceous leaves. Slightly
fragrant.*

MISS FRANCE
*('Pretty Girl') by Gaujard, 1955. Parentage: 'Peace' ×
'Independence'. Vigorous; large, double, globular corollas,
bronzy leaves. Fragrant.*

MISS IRELAND
*('Macir') by S. McGredy IV, 1961. Parentage: 'Tzigane'
× 'Independence'. Vigorous, bushy; large corollas of 37
petals, orange with yellow underside, dark leaves. Fragrant.*

MISS SATSUKI
*by A. Kimoto, 1978. Large corollas of 33 petals, creamy
pink edged coral-pink.*

MISS UNIVERSE
*by Gaujard, 1956. Parentage: ('Peace' × seedling) ×
seedling. Vigorous; large, double corollas, orange with
underside flushed bronze, dark leaves. Fragrant.*

MR. LINCOLN
*('Mister Lincoln') by Swim & Weeks, 1964. Parentage:
'Chrysler Imperial' × 'Charles Mallerin'. Vigorous; large
corollas of 35 petals, turbinate to cupped, urn-shaped buds,
opaque, coriaceous, dark leaves. Very fragrant. All-America
Rose Selections award, 1965.*

Miss Satsuki

Miss Universe

Mr. Lincoln

Mrs. Henry Morse

Mrs. Herbert Stevens

Mrs. Oakley Fisher

Miwaku

Mrs. Sam McGredy

Miyabi

Miyako Ooji

Mizuho

MRS. HENRY MORSE
by McGredy, 1919. Dwarf growth; large, double corollas, creamy white suffused with pink-veined red, tapered buds. Fragrant. Gold Medal Royal National Rose Society, 1919.

MRS. HERBERT STEVENS
by McGredy, 1910. Parentage: 'Frau Karl Druschki' × 'Niphetos'. Bushy; double corollas, pointed buds, light leaves.

MRS. OAKLEY FISHER
by B. R. Cant. Vigorous; single corollas of 5 petals, dark, bronzy leaves.

MRS. SAM MCGREDY
by McGredy, 1929. Parentage: ('Donald Macdonald' × 'Golden Emblem') × (seedling × 'The Queen Alexandra Rose'). Vigorous; large corollas of 40 petals, pointed buds, glossy, bronzy leaves. Fragrant. Gold Medal Royal National Rose Society, 1929.

MIWAKU
by S. Suzuki, 1988. Parentage: 'White Masterpiece' × 'Confidence'. Corollas of 15 petals, creamy white edged pink. Fragrant.

MIYABI
by K. Teranishi, 1977. Parentage: ('Amatsu Otome' × 'Samba') × ('Kordes' Perfecta' × 'American Heritage'). Upright; large corollas of 30 petals, ovoid buds. Slightly fragrant.

MIYAKO OOJI
by Keihan Hirakata, 1988. Corollas deep pink with lighter underside. Slightly fragrant.

MIZUHO
by T. Tanaka, 1970. Parentage: 'Izayoi' × 'Kordes' Perfecta'. Corollas with pointed petals, soft pink especially light in spring.

Modern Times

MODERN TIMES
by Verbeek, 1956. Parentage: sport of 'Better Times'.
Corollas red, striped with pink.

MOMOYAMA
by Keihan Hirakata, 1981. Parentage: 'Helen Traubel' ×
'Ann Letts'. Corollas of 35–40 petals, pink on
orange-yellow base.

MONIKA
('Tanaknom') by M. Tantau, 1985. Parentage unknown.
Upright; medium corollas of 35 petals, glossy, dark leaves.
Slightly fragrant.

MONTE CARLO
by F. Meilland, 1949. Parentage: 'Peace' × seedling.
Corollas gold-yellow, edged red.

MOUNT SHASTA
by Swim & Weeks, 1963. Parentage: 'Queen Elizabeth' ×
'Charles Mallerin'. Vigorous, upright; large, double, cupped
corollas, tapered and pointed buds, green-gray, coriaceous
leaves. Fragrant.

MY CHOICE
by Le Grice, 1958. Parentage: 'Wellworth' × 'Ena
Harkness'. Vigorous, upright; large corollas of 33 petals,
pink with light yellow underside, coriaceous leaves. Strong
damascena fragrance. Gold Medal Royal National Rose
Society, 1958, and Portland, 1961.

NATIONAL TRUST
('Bad Naukeim') by S. McGredy IV, 1970. Parentage:
'Evelyn Fison' × 'King of Hearts'. Large corollas of 53
petals, classic form.

Momoyama

Mount Shasta

Monika

My Choice

Monte Carlo

National Trust

Neige Parfum

New Carina

Neue Revue

New Style

New Year

New Yorker

Nocturne

Norita

Oh-Choh

NEIGE PARFUM
by Mallerini, 1942. Parentage: 'Joanna Hill' × ('White Ophelia' × seedling). Vigorous; large, double corollas, white, sometimes cream, coriaceous leaves. Very fragrant.

NEUE REVUE
('Korrev') by Kordes, 1962. Parentage: 'Colour Wonder' × unknown. Upright; large, well-formed corollas of 30 petals, yellow to white touched dark red, coriaceous leaves, large and numerous prickles. Very fragrant.

NEW YEAR
('Macnewye', 'Arcadian') by S. McGredy, 1983. Parentage: 'Mary Summer' × unnamed seedling. Upright, compact; medium corollas of 20 petals, burnt orange and gold, large, dark, glossy leaves. Slightly fragrant. Also classified among the Grandiflora. All-America Rose Selections award, 1987.

NEW CARINA
by C. Yokota, 1975. Parentage: sport of Carina. Corollas of 35–40 petals, cyclamen-pink.

NEW STYLE
by A. Meilland, 1972. Parentage: ('Happiness' × 'Independence') × 'Peace'. Corollas of 30 petals, deep red.

NEW YORKER
by Boerner, 1947. Parentage: 'Flambeau' × seedling. Vigorous and bushy; large corollas of 35 petals. Fruity fragrance.

NOCTURNE
by Swim, 1947. Parentage: 'Charlotte Armstrong' × 'Night'. Upright, vigorous, bushy; large, cupped corollas of 24 petals, tapered buds, small, light green, glossy leaves. Spicy fragrance. All-America Rose Selections award, 1948.

NORITA
by Combe, 1971. Parentage: 'Charles Mallerin' × seedling. Vigorous, bushy; large, double corollas, dark, coriaceous leaves. Fragrant.

OH-CHOH
by S. Suzuki, 1983. Parentage: ('Rumba' × 'Olympic Torch') × 'Wisbech Gold'. Upright; large corollas of 38 petals, yellow tinted pink turning red, dark, semiglossy leaves, small prickles slanted downward.

OREGOLD
('Miss Harp', 'Silhouette', 'Anneliesse Rottenberger') by Tantau, 1975. Parentage: 'Piccadilly' × 'Color Wonder'. Vigorous, upright, bushy; large, double, turbinate corollas, deep yellow, large, dark, glossy leaves. All-America Rose Selections award, 1975.

OKLAHOMA
by Swim & Weeks, 1964. Parentage: 'Chrysler Imperial' × 'Charles Mallerin'. Vigorous, bushy; large corollas of 48 petals, ovoid, pointed buds, dark, opaque, coriaceous leaves. Very fragrant. Gold Medal Tokyo, 1963.

OLÉ
by D. L. Armstrong, 1964. Parentage: 'Roundelay' × 'El Capitan'. Corollas of 45 petals, vermilion.

OPERA
by Gaujard, 1950. Parentage: 'La Belle Irisée' × seedling. Vigorous, upright; large, double corollas, scarlet on a yellow base, light green, coriaceous leaves. Fragrant. Gold Medal Royal National Rose Society, 1949.

OPHELIA
by W. Paul, 1912. Parentage unknown; perhaps derived from 'Antoine Rivoire'. Vigorous; corollas of 28 petals, flesh-colored with yellow center, tapered and pointed buds, coriaceous leaves. Fragrant.

ORANGE DELBARD
by Delbard-Chabert, 1959. Parentage: 'Impeccable' × 'Mme. Robert Joffet'.

Oregold

Oklahoma

Olé

Orange Delbard

Opera

Ophelia

Oriana

Osiria

Otohime

Papa Meilland

Paradise

ORIANA
by Tantau, 1970. Large corollas of 38 petals, cherry with white underside, glossy and dark leaves. Slightly fragrant.

OSIRIA
by W. Kordes, 1978. Parentage: 'Snowfire' × seedling. Upright, vigorous, bushy; large corollas of 50 petals, dark red with white underside on short steles, tapered buds. Very fragrant.

OTOHIME
('Fancy Princess') by Keisei Rose Nursery, 1977. Parentage: ('Hawaii' × 'Tropicana') × ('Tropicana' × 'Peace'). Vigorous; very large corollas of 58 petals, pointed buds, large, dark, glossy leaves. Fragrant.

PAPA MEILLAND
('Meisar') by Alain Meilland, 1963. Parentage: 'Chrysler Imperial' × 'Charles Mallerin'. Vigorous, upright; large corollas of 35 petals, pointed buds, coriaceous, glossy, olive-green leaves. Very fragrant. Gold Medal Baden Baden, 1962.

PARADISE
('Wezeip', 'Burning Sky') by Weeks, 1978. Parentage: 'Swarthmore' × seedling. Upright; large, well-formed corollas of 28 petals, silvery lavender edged ruby red, dark, glossy leaves. Fragrant. All-America Rose Selections award, 1979.

Pariser Charme

Parthenon

Party Dress

Pascali

Pasadena

PARISER CHARME
by M. Tantau, 1965. Large corollas, slightly rippling petals, pink, flushed with coral.

PARTHENON
('Delbro') by Delbard-Chabert, 1967. Parentage: 'Chic Parisien' × ('Bayadère' × 'Rome Glory').

PARTY DRESS
by H. Robinson, 1961. Parentage: 'Gay Cruzader' × seedling. Vigorous, bushy, compact; large corollas of 25 petals, glossy leaves. Fragrant.

PASADENA
('Korland') by W. Kordes, 1981. Parentage: 'Mercedes' × ('Sweet Promise' × ('Miss Ireland' × 'Zorina')).

PASCALI
('Lenip') by Lens, 1963. Parentage: 'Queen Elizabeth' × 'White Butterfly'.

PEACE
('Gioia', 'Gloria Dei', 'Mme. A. Meilland') by F. Meilland, 1945. Parentage: (('George Dickson' × 'Souvenir de Claudius Pernet') × ('Joanna Hill' × 'Charles P. Kilham')) × 'Margaret McGredy'.

Peace

Peer Gynt

Peter Frankenfeld

Percy Thrower

Pfälzer Gold

Perfume Delight

Pharaoh

Piccadilly

Picnica

PEER GYNT
('Korol') by R. Kordes, 1968. Parentage: 'Colour Wonder' × 'Golden Giant'. Vigorous, bushy; large corollas of 50 petals, retroflexing, yellow edged with red. Slightly fragrant. Gold Medal Belfast, 1970.

PERCY THROWER
by Lens, 1964. Parentage: 'La Jolla' × 'Karl Herbst'. Tall, vigorous; large, well-formed corollas of 28 petals, glossy leaves. Fragrant.

PERFUME DELIGHT
by Weeks, 1973. Parentage: 'Peace' × (('Happiness' × 'Chrysler Imperial') × 'El Capitan'). Vigorous, upright, bushy; large, double, cupped corollas, large, coriaceous leaves. Very fragrant. All-America Rose Selections award, 1974.

PETER FRANKENFELD
by R. Kordes, 1966. Large, well-formed corollas. Slightly fragrant.

PFÄLZER GOLD
by M. Tantau, 1981. Corollas of 40 petals, yellow.

PHARAOH
('Meifiga', 'Pharaon') by M. L. Meilland, 1967. Parentage: ('Happiness' × 'Independence') × 'Suspense'. Vigorous, upright; large, double corollas, ovoid buds, dark, glossy, coriaceous leaves. Fragrant. Gold Medal Geneva, Madrid, and The Hague, 1967, Belfast, 1968.

PICCADILLY
by S. McGredy IV, 1960. Parentage: 'McGredy's Yellow' × 'Karl Herbst'. Vigorous and upright, branched growth; large, long, and pointed corollas of 28 petals, scarlet on a gold base with gold underside, dark and glossy leaves. Gold Medal Madrid and Rome, 1960.

PICNICA
by K. Ota, 1977. Parentage: 'Edith Krause' × 'Bridal Robe'. Corollas of 30–35 petals, cream flushed with white.

PINK LUSTRE

by Verschuren, 1957. Parentage: 'Peace' × 'Dame Edith Helen'. Vigorous and upright; large corollas of 48 petals, ovoid buds, dark, coriaceous, glossy leaves. Very fragrant.

PINK PANTHER

('Meicapina') by M. L. Meilland, 1981. Parentage: 'Meigurami' × 'Meinaregi'. Upright; large corollas of 40 petals and more, silvery pink edged glowing pink, semiglossy leaves. No fragrance.

PINK PARFAIT

by Swim, 1960. Parentage: 'First Love' × 'Pinocchio'. Vigorous, upright, bushy; large corollas of 23 petals, turbinate to cupped, outer petals pink, center suffused orange, ovoid to urn-shaped buds, semiglossy leaves. Slightly fragrant. Gold Medal Baden Baden and Portland, 1959, Royal National Rose Society, 1962, All-America Rose Selections award, 1961. Placed by many authors among the Grandiflora.

PINK PEACE

('Meibil') by F. Meilland, 1959. Parentage: ('Peace' × 'Monique') × ('Peace' × 'Mrs. John Laing'). Tall, vigorous, bushy; large corollas of 58 petals, coriaceous leaves. Very fragrant. Gold Medal Geneva and Rome, 1959.

POLYNESIAN SUNSET

by Boerner, 1965. Parentage: 'Diamond Jubilee' seedling × 'Hawaii'. Vigorous, bushy; large corollas, tapered buds, coriaceous leaves. Fruity fragrance.

PORTRAIT

('Meypink', 'Stéphanie de Monaco') by C. Meyer, 1971. Parentage: 'Pink Parfait' × 'Pink Peace'. Upright, bushy; medium, double corollas, ovoid buds, dark, glossy leaves. Fragrant. Amateur winner, All-America Rose Selections, 1972.

PRECIOUS PLATINUM

('Opa Potschke', 'Red Star') by Dicksons of Hawlmark, 1974. Parentage: 'Red Planet' × 'Frankl in Engelmann'. Medium to large, full corollas, coriaceous, glossy leaves. Slightly fragrant.

PRELUDE

('Sugar Plum') by Swim, 1954. Parentage: 'Crimson Glory' × 'Girona'. Vigorous, upright, bushy; large corollas of 55 petals, turbinate to flat, ovoid buds, glossy, coriaceous, dark leaves. Spicy fragrance.

Pink Lustre

Pink Panther

Pink Parfait

Pink Peace

Portrait

Precious Platinum

Polynesian Sunset

Prelude

Premier Bal

Preziosa

President Leopold Senghor

Prima Ballerina

PREMIER BAL
by F. Meilland, 1955. Parentage: ('Fantastique' × 'Caprice') × 'Peace'. Large corollas of 25–30 petals, cream white edged with fuchsia. Intense fragrance.

PRESIDENT HERBERT HOOVER
by Coddington, 1930. Parentage: 'Sensation' × 'Souvenir de Claudius Pernet'. Tall, vigorous; large corollas of 25 petals, orange, pink, and gold with lighter underside, coriaceous leaves. Spicy fragrance. Two American Rose Society awards, 1935.

PRESIDENT LEOPOLD SENGHOR
('Meiluminac') by M. L. Meilland, 1979. Parentage: (('Scarlet Knight' × 'Samourai') × ('Crimson Wave' × 'Imperator') × ('Pharaoh' × 'Pharaoh')) × ('Pharaoh' × 'Pharaoh'). Vigorous, bushy; large, full, and cupped corollas, conical buds, dark, glossy leaves.

PREZIOSA
('Indian Song', 'Meihimper') by Meilland, 1971. Parentage: ('Radar' × 'Karl Herbst') × 'Sabrina'. Vigorous, upright; large corollas of 40 petals, pink, with reverse gold, dark, glossy leaves. Slightly fragrant.

PRIMA BALLERINA
('Première Ballerine') by M. Tantau, 1957. Parentage: unknown × 'Peace'. Medium to large corollas of 20 petals, tapered and pointed buds, light green, coriaceous leaves. Very fragrant.

President Herbert Hoover

Princesse de Monaco

Pristine

Princess Sayako

Princess Takamatsu

Prominent

Promise

Queen Elizabeth

PRINCESSE DE MONACO
('Meimagarmi', 'Grace Kelly', 'Preference') by M. L.
Meilland, 1981. Parentage: 'Ambassador' × 'Peace'.
Upright, bushy; large corollas of 35 petals, cream-edged
pink, large, dark, glossy leaves. Fragrant.

PRINCESS SAYAKO
by M. L. Meilland, 1980. Parentage: sport of 'Candia'.
Corollas of 30 petals, salmon-pink-edged deep pink on a
cream base.

PRINCESS TAKAMATSU
by K. Kono, 1974. Parentage: 'Bonsoir' × 'Christian
Dior'. Corollas of 50 petals, cream white on a soft orange
base. Slightly fragrant.

PRISTINE
('Jacpico') by Warriner, 1978. Parentage: 'White
Masterpiece' × 'First Prize'. Upright; large, imbricated
corollas of 28 petals, white-tinted light pink, tapered buds,
very large, dark leaves. Slightly fragrant.

PROMINENT
('Korp') by R. Kordes, 1971. Parentage: 'Colour Wonder'
× 'Zorina'. Upright; large, cupped corollas of 33 petals,
tapered and pointed buds, opaque leaves. Slightly fragrant.
Gold Medal Portland and All-America Rose Selections
award, 1977.

PROMISE
('Poesie') by Warriner, 1976. Parentage: 'South Seas' ×
'Peace'. Vigorous; large, double corollas, large and glossy
leaves. Slightly fragrant.

QUEEN ELIZABETH
by Lammerts, 1954. Parentage: 'Charlotte Armstrong' ×
'Floradora'. Very vigorous, upright, bushy; large corollas of
38 petals, turbinate to cupped, dark, coriaceous, glossy
leaves. Fragrant. Gold Medal Royal National Rose Society,
1955, and American Rose Society, 1960, All-America
Rose Selections award, 1955, Golden Rose of The Hague,
1968. Placed by some authors among the Grandiflora.

RADIANCE
('Pink Radiance') by J. Cook. 1908. Parentage:
'Enchanter' × 'Cardinal'. Vigorous; large, cupped corollas
of 23 petals, globular buds, coriaceous leaves. Strong
damascena fragrance.

RAINBOW SUNSET
Author unknown. Parentage: sport of 'Piccadilly'. Corollas
of 25 petals, red streaked yellow. Slightly fragrant.

RED DEVIL
('Dicam', 'Coeur d'Amour') by A. Dickson, 1970.
Parentage: 'Silver Lining' × 'Prima Ballerina'. Vigorous;
very double, large corollas of 72 petals, ovoid buds, glossy
leaves. Fragrant. Gold Medal Tokyo, 1967, and Belfast,
1969.

RED LION
by S. McGredy IV, 1964. Parentage: 'Kordes' Perfecta' ×
'Detroiter'. Large corollas of 38 petals.

RED PLANET
by P. Dickson, 1970. Parentage: 'Red Devil' × seedling.
Large corollas of 30 petals, glossy leaves. Very fragrant. Gold
Medal Royal National Rose Society, 1960.

RED QUEEN
('Liebestraum') by Kordes, 1968. Parentage: 'Colour
Wonder' × 'Liberty Bell'. Upright and vigorous; large,
double corollas, ovoid buds, dark leaves.

RED SUCCESS
by Meilland, 1980. Corollas of 35–40 petals, vermilion.

RENDEZ-VOUS
('Day of Triumph') by F. Meilland, 1953. Parentage:
'Peace' × 'Europa'. Vigorous, upright, bushy; large, cupped
corollas of 60 petals, ovoid buds, coriaceous leaves. Fragrant.

REX ANDERSON
by McGredy, 1938. Parentage: 'Florence L. Izzard' ×
'Mrs. Charles Lamplough'. Vigorous, timid bloom; double,
very well-formed corollas, gray-green leaves. Fruity fragrance.

Radiance

Rainbow Sunset

Red Devil

Red Lion

Red Success

Red Planet

Rendez-vous

Red Queen

Rex Anderson

Romantica '76

Rouge Meilland

Rose Fukuoka

Royal Albert Hall

Rose Gaujard

Royal Highness

ROMANTICA '76
by Meilland, 1976. Corollas of 25 petals, orange-pink.

ROSE FUKUOKA
by K. Ota, 1983. Parentage: ('Utage' × 'Kordes' Perfecta')
× 'Miss Ireland'. Compact growth; large corollas of 27
petals, small, dark, and glossy leaves. Slightly fragrant.

ROSE GAUJARD
('Gaumo') by Gaujard, 1957. Parentage: 'Peace' ×
'Opera' seedling. Vigorous, bushy; large corollas of 80
petals, turbinate to cupped, cherry with light pink and silver
underside, coriaceous, glossy leaves. Slightly fragrant. Gold
Medal Royal National Rose Society, 1958.

ROUGE MEILLAND
('Happiness') by F. Meilland, 1949. Parentage: ('Rome
Glory' × 'Tassin') × ('Charles P. Kilham' × ('Charles
P. Kilham' × 'Capucine Chambard')). Upright, vigorous;
large corollas of 38 petals, tapered and pointed buds. Slightly
fragrant.

ROYAL ALBERT HALL
by Cocker, 1972. Parentage: 'Fragrant Cloud' × 'Postillon'.
Large corollas of 32 petals, wine red with gold underside,
dark leaves. Very fragrant.

ROYAL HIGHNESS
('Königliche Hoheit') by Swim & Weeks, 1962. Parentage:
'Virgo' × 'Peace'. Bushy and upright, suited to temperate
climates; large corollas of 43 petals, tapered and pointed
buds, dark, glossy, and coriaceous leaves. Very fragrant. Gold
Medal Portland, 1960, Madrid, 1962, All-America Rose
Selections award, 1963, and American Rose Society, 1964.

SABRINA
by M. L. Meilland, 1960. Parentage: 'Grand Gala' ×
'Premier Bal'. Vigorous, bushy; large corollas of 35 petals,
crimson with amber underside marked crimson, dark,
coriaceous leaves. Very fragrant.

SAGANO
by K. Hirakata, 1982. Parentage: 'Kinkaku' × 'Takano'.

SAI-UN
by S. Suzuki, 1980. Parentage: ('Miss All-American
Beauty' × 'Kagayaki') × seedling. Upright; large corollas
of 50 petals, dark, glossy leaves, prickles slanted downward.
Fragrant.

Sabrina

Sagano

Sai-Un

SAMANTHA
('Jacmantha') by Warriner, 1974. Parentage: 'Bridal Pink' × seedling. Upright, vigorous; medium, double corollas, coriaceous leaves. Slightly fragrant.

SAMOURAI
('Scarlet Knight', 'Meielec') by M. L. Meilland, 1966. Parentage: ('Happiness' × 'Independence') × 'Sutter's Gold'. Vigorous, upright, bushy; large, cupped, double corollas, ovoid buds, coriaceous leaves. Slightly fragrant. Gold Medal Madrid, 1966, All-America Rose Selections award, 1968.

SANDRA
('Sandkor') by Kordes, 1981. Parentage: 'Mercedes' × seedling. Upright; large corollas of 35 petals, medium green, opaque leaves. Slightly fragrant.

SAN FRANCISCO
by Lammerts, 1962. Parentage: 'Dean Collins' × 'Independence'. Vigorous, compact, and branched growth; large corollas of 40 petals, turbinate to cupped, ovoid buds, dark, glossy, coriaceous leaves. Fragrant.

SANKA
by S. Suzuki, 1986. Parentage: 'Todoroki' × 'Ave Maria'. Corollas of 35 petals, soft coral when young then deeper colored. Slightly fragrant.

SATOMI
by M. Suga, 1969. Parentage: sport of 'Christian Dior'. Corollas with pointed petals, fuchsia-pink.

SATURNIA
by D. Aicardi, 1936. Parentage: 'Julien Potin' × 'Sensation'. Vigorous; large, cupped corollas of 20 petals, scarlet to gold, dark and glossy leaves. Fruity fragrance. Gold Medal Rome, 1933, Portland, 1938.

SCHWEIZER GOLD
by Kordes, 1975. Parentage: 'Peer Gynt' × 'King's Ransom'. Vigorous; double corollas, ovoid buds, light leaves. Fragrant. Gold Medal Baden Baden, 1972.

Samantha

Samourai

Sandra

San Francisco

Satomi

Sanka

Schweizer Gold

Saturnia

Seika

Seikoh

Seiryoden

Seki-Yoh

Seventh Heaven

Shannon

SEIKA
('Olympic Torch') by S. Suzuki, 1966. Parentage: 'Rose Gaujard' × 'Crimson Glory'. Vigorous; medium, double corollas, white and red then entirely red, tapered buds, bronzy, glossy, coriaceous leaves. Gold Medal New Zealand, 1971.

SEIKOH
by S. Suzuki, 1975. Parentage: ('Sarabande' × 'Amanogawa') × 'Kronenbourg'. Corollas of 30–35 petals, deep yellow.

SEIRYODEN
by K. Kuroda, 1961. Parentage: 'Ulster Monarch' × 'McGredy's Ivory'. Large corollas, cream white flushed and edged pink. Very fragrant.

SEKI-YOH
by S. Suzuki, 1965. Parentage: 'Miss France' × 'Christian Dior'. Upright and compact; large corollas of 52 petals, dark, coriaceous, semiglossy leaves. Slightly fragrant.

SEVENTH HEAVEN
by D. L. Armstrong and Swim, 1966. Parentage: seedling × 'Chrysler Imperial'. Upright, bushy; large, double corollas, glossy leaves.

SHANNON
('Macnon') by S. McGredy IV, 1965. Parentage: 'Queen Elizabeth' × 'McGredy Yellow'. Vigorous; large corollas of 58 petals, ovoid buds, dark, rounded leaves.

SHINJU
by Toshiyuki Harada, 1976. Parentage: 'Royal Highness' × 'Garden Party'. Vigorous, upright; large corollas of 28 petals, coriaceous, medium green leaves, many prickles slanted downward. Fragrant.

SHIN-SEI
by S. Suzuki, 1969. Parentage: ('Ethel Sanday' × 'Lydia') × 'Koto'. Upright, bushy; large, well-formed corollas of 38 petals, tapered buds, large, medium green, glossy leaves, prickles pointed downward. Fragrant.

SHIRALEE
by P. Dickson, 1965. Parentage: seedling × 'Kordes' Perfecta'. Tall, vigorous; large corollas of 36 petals, yellow suffused orange. Fragrant. Gold Medal Tokyo, 1964.

SHI-UN
by S. Suzuki, 1984. Parentage: ('Blue Moon' × 'Twilight') × ('Red American Beauty' × 'Happiness'). Vigorous, upright, bushy; medium corollas of 33 petals, lilac purple with deeper colored underside, dark, coriaceous, semiglossy leaves, prickles slanted downward. Fragrant.

SHOW GIRL
by Lammerts, 1946. Parentage: 'Joanna Hill' × 'Crimson Glory'. Vigorous, upright, bushy; large corollas of 15–20 petals, tapered buds, coriaceous leaves. Fragrant. Gold Medal Royal National Rose Society, 1950.

SHOWSTOPPER
by Warriner, 1981. Parentage: seedling × 'Samantha'. Robust, bushy; corollas of 33 petals, large leaves, long prickles. Slightly fragrant.

SHU-GETSU
by S. Suzuki, 1982. Parentage: 'Seiko' × 'King's Ransom'. Upright, bushy; large corollas of 38 petals, large, dark, glossy leaves, large, straight prickles. Fragrant.

Shinju

Shin-sei

Shiralee

Show Girl

Showstopper

Shi-un

Shu-getsu

Shunpo

Silhouette

Shu-oh

Sierra Dawn

SHUNPO
by Keisei Rose Nursery. 1987. Parentage: 'Perfume Delight' × ('Blue Moon' × 'Intermezzo'). Corollas pink. Fragrant.

SHU-OH
by S. Suzuki, 1982. Parentage: 'San Francisco' × 'Pharaoh'. Upright; medium, cupped corollas, dark, semiglossy leaves, prickles slanted downward. Fragrant.

SIERRA DAWN
by D. L. Armstrong, 1967. Parentage: 'Helen Traubel' × 'Manitou'. Vigorous, upright, bushy; large, double corollas, tapered and pointed buds, bronzy, dark, coriaceous leaves. Fragrant.

SILHOUETTE
('Silver Medal') by Warriner, 1980. Upright; large corollas of 25 petals, white edged pink, tapered buds, light leaves.

SILVA
('Meicham') by A. Meilland, 1964. Parentage: 'Peace' × 'Confidence'. Large corollas of 15–35 petals, salmon-pink flushed yellow. Gold Medal The Hague, 1964.

Silva

Silver Lining

Simona

Silver Star

Sodõhri-himé

Simon Bolivar

Solidor

Sonia

Sonja Horstmann

Souma

SILVER LINING
by A. Dickson, 1958. Parentage: 'Karl Herbst' × 'Eden Rose' seedling. Vigorous; large corollas of 30 petals, silvery pink. Very fragrant. Gold Medal Royal National Rose Society, 1958.

SILVER STAR
('Korbido') by R. Kordes, 1966. Parentage: 'Sterling Silver' × 'Magenta' seedling. Large, well-formed, double corollas, dark leaves. Very fragrant.

SIMON BOLIVAR
by D. L. Armstrong, 1966. Parentage: 'Roundelay' × 'El Capitan'. Upright, vigorous, bushy; large corollas of 40 petals, ovoid buds, dark, coriaceous, glossy leaves. Slightly fragrant.

SIMONA
('Tanmosina') by M. Tantau, 1979. Parentage unknown. Greenhouse variety; large corollas of 20 petals, large, medium green, opaque leaves. Fragrant.

SODÕHRI-HIMÉ
('La Blancheur') by T. Onodera, 1975. Parentage: 'White Knight' × 'White Prince'. Bushy; large corollas of 30 petals, dark leaves. Slightly fragrant.

SOLIDOR
by Meilland, 1985. Corollas of 25–30 petals, deep yellow.

SONIA
('Meihelvet', 'Sonia Meilland', 'Sweet Promise'), by Meilland, 1974. Parentage: 'Zambra' × ('Baccará' × 'White Knight'). Large corollas of 30 petals, pink-flushed coral blue, tapered buds, glossy, dark, coriaceous leaves. Strong, fruity fragrance.

SONJA HORSTMANN
by Kordes, 1967. Corollas of 25 petals, red.

SOUMA
by Souma Rose Soc., 1977. Parentage unknown. Upright and vigorous; large corollas of 45 petals, dark and glossy leaves. Slightly fragrant.

Souv. du President Plumecocq

Sujaku

Star Queen

Sterling

SOUVENIR DU PRESIDENT PLUMECOCQ
by Laperrière, 1958. Parentage: seedling × 'Peace'. Large corollas, scarlet-flushed silver. Fragrant.

STAR QUEEN
by A. Kaneko, 1963. Parentage: 'Poinsettia' × 'Show Girl'.

STERLING
by E. G. Hill Co., 1933. Parentage: 'Mme. Butterfly' × seedling. Vigorous; large corollas of 35 petals, bright pink on yellow base, glossy leaves. Fragrant. Gold Medal Portland, 1938, and American Rose Society, 1939.

STERLING SILVER
by G. Fisher, 1957. Parentage: seedling × 'Peace'. Upright and vigorous; medium corollas of 30 petals, turbinate to cupped, dark and glossy leaves. Very fragrant.

SUJAKU
by K. Hirakata, 1977. Parentage: 'Hawaii' × seed plant. Corollas of 30–35 petals, deep orange. Slightly fragrant.

Sterling Silver

SUMA NO URA
by K. Teranishi, 1980. Parentage: ('Rob Roi' ×
'Himatsuri') × seedling. Medium height, bushy; medium
corollas of 40 petals, small, medium green, semiglossy leaves,
large, reddish-brown prickles. No fragrance.

SUMMER DREAM
('Jacshe') by Warriner, 1987. Upright, tall; medium
corollas of 30 petals, apricot, medium green, opaque leaves.

SUMMER HOLIDAY
by Gregory, 1967. Parentage: 'Tropicana' × unknown.
Very vigorous; corollas of 48 petals, semiglossy leaves.
Fragrant.

SUMMER SUNSHINE
('Soleil d'Été') by Swim, 1962. Parentage: 'Buccaneer' ×
'Lemon Chiffon'. Vigorous, upright, well branched; corollas
of 25 petals, turbinate to cupped, ovoid buds, coriaceous,
dark, semiglossy leaves. Slightly fragrant.

SUN KING
by F. Meilland, 1954. Parentage: 'Peace' × 'Duchesse de
Talleyrand'. Vigorous, upright; large corollas of 45 petals,
tapered buds, dark, glossy, coriaceous leaves. Fragrant.

SUNBRIGHT
by Warriner, 1984. Parentage: seedling × 'New Day'.
Upright; large corollas of 28 petals, flat, tapered buds.
Slightly fragrant.

SUPER STAR
('Tropicana', 'Tanorstar') by M. Tantau, 1960. Vigorous,
upright; large, well-formed corollas of 33 petals, pointed
buds, dark, glossy, coriaceous leaves. Strong fruit fragrance.
Gold Medal Royal National Rose Society, 1960,
All-America Rose Selections, 1963, American Rose Society,
1967.

SUPREME
by Le Grice, 1966. Parentage: 'Golden Masterpiece' ×
'Ethel Sanday'. Large corollas, cream colored in mild
climates, yellow in cold climates.

SUSAN HAMPSHIRE
('Meinatac') by Paolino, 1972. Parentage: ('Monique' ×
'Symphonie') × 'Miss All-American Beauty'. Vigorous,
upright; large, globular corollas of 40 petals, opaque leaves.

Suma no Ura

Summer Dream

Summer Holiday

Summer Sunshine

Super Star

Sunbright

Supreme

Sun King

Susan Hampshire

Tahiti

Tournament of Roses

TAHITI
by F. Meilland, 1947. Parentage: 'Peace' × 'Signora'.
Large, double corollas, amber-flushed carmine, dark, glossy
leaves. Very fragrant.

TAKAO
by K. Okamoto, 1975. Parentage: ('Masquerade' ×
'Lydia') × ('Montezuma' × 'Miss Ireland'). Medium
height, bushy; medium corollas of 33 petals, medium green
leaves, dark brown prickles. Damascena fragrance.

TATJANA
('Kortat') by R. Kordes, 1970. Parentage: 'Liebeszauber' ×
'Präsident Dr. H. C. Schroeder'. Vigorous, upright; large,
cupped, double corollas, soft leaves.

TIFFANY
by Lindquist, 1954. Parentage: 'Charlotte Armstrong' ×
'Girona'. Vigorous and erect; large corollas of 28 petals,
dark leaves. Very fragrant. All-America Rose Selections
award, 1955, American Rose Society, 1957, Rose
Fragrance Medal, 1962.

Tiffany

Touch of Class

Takao

Tatjana

TODOROKI
*by Keisei Rose Nurseries, 1977. Parentage: ('Pharaoh' ×
'Kagayaki') × 'Yu-Ai'. Vigorous; large corollas of 33
petals, pointed buds, dark leaves. Slight fragrance.*

TOUCH OF CLASS
*('Kricarlo', 'Marechal le Clerc') by M. Kriloff, 1984.
Parentage: 'Michaela' × ('Queen Elizabeth' ×
'Romantica'). Double corollas of 33 petals, pink, large,
dark, and glossy leaves. Slightly fragrant. All-America Rose
Selections, 1986.*

TOURNAMENT OF ROSES
*by Warriner, 1988. Parentage: 'Impatient' × unnamed
seedling. Corollas of pink shades in small, numerous
bunches. This rose commemorates the centennial of the
Tournament of Roses. Also classified among the Grandiflora.
All-America Rose Selections, 1989.*

TOWN CRIER
*by J. H. Hill Co., 1961. Parentage: 'Peace' × 'Yellow
Perfection'. Vigorous, erect, well branched; large corollas of
33 petals, ovoid buds, dark, shiny leaves. Fragrant.*

Todoroki

Town Crier

Triumph

Utage

Tzigane

Utamaro

Ulster Monarch

Utano

Valiant

Vega

Victor Hugo

TRIUMPH
by Kordes, 1971. Corollas of 15 petals, scarlet with ivory underside.

TZIGANE
by F. Meilland, 1951. Parentage: 'Peace' × 'J. B. Meilland'. Erect, bushy; large, double corollas cup-shaped and in the form of cacti, pink with yellow undersides, dark, coriaceous, shiny leaves. Fragrant.

ULSTER MONARCH
by McGredy, 1951. Parentage: 'Sam McGredy' × 'Mrs. Sam McGredy' by seedling. Erect; medium corollas, pointed, of 50 petals, brilliant green, shiny leaves. Fragrant.

UTAGE
by S. Suzuki, 1979. Parentage: 'Chicago Peace' × 'Kagayaki'. Corollas of 25–28 petals, scarlet with lighter underside.

UTAMARO
by S. Suzuki, 1973. Parentage: ('Queen Elizabeth' × 'Pink Peace') × 'Peace'. Large corollas of 35 petals, fuchsia pink.

UTANO
by Keihan Hirakata Nursery, 1985. Parentage: 'Takao' × 'Kinkaku'. Corollas of 50 petals, yellow-flushed orange-pink. Slightly fragrant.

VALIANT
by Boerner, 1948. Parentage: 'Poinsettia' × 'Satan'. Vigorous, erect, and well-branched; large corollas of 30 petals, dark, coriaceous leaves. Fragrant.

VEGA
by Meilland, 1976. Parentage: 'Forever Yours' × 'Love Affair'. Large corollas of 25 petals, scarlet. Fragrant buds.

VICTOR HUGO
by Meilland, 1985. Corollas of 35 petals, dark red. Fragrant.

Virgo

White Christmas

Wendy Cussons

Western Sun

VIRGO
('Virgo Liberationem') by Mallerin, 1947. Parentage: 'Blanche Mallerin' × 'Neige Parfum'. Vigorous; large corollas of 30 petals, dark, coriaceous leaves. Slight fragrance. Gold Medal Royal National Rose Society, 1949.

WENDY CUSSONS
by Gregory, 1973. Parentage: 'Independence' × 'Eden Rose'. Vigorous, branching; large corollas of 30 petals, tapered and pointed buds, dark, shiny, and coriaceous leaves. Very fragrant. Certificate of Merit Royal Horticultural Society, 1959, Golden Rose The Hague, 1964, Gold Medal Portland, 1964.

WESTERN SUN
by N. D. Poulsen, 1965. Parentage: 'Golden Scepter' by seedling × 'Golden Sun'. Large corollas of 40 petals, dark leaves.

WHITE CHRISTMAS
by Howard & Smith, 1953. Parentage: 'Sleigh Bells' × seed plant. Medium height, erect; medium, double corollas, tapered and pointed buds, light green, coriaceous leaves. Fragrant.

WHITE MASTERPIECE
by Boerner, 1969. Erect; very large, double corollas, tapered and pointed buds. Slight fragrance.

White Masterpiece

WHITE PRINCE
by Von Abrams, 1961. Parentage: ('Blanche Mallerin' × 'Peace') × ('Peace' × 'Frau Karl Drushki').

WHITE WINGS
by Krebs, 1947. Parentage: 'Dainty Bess' × seed plant. Vigorous, erect, bushy; single corollas of 5 petals, medium size in large bunches, white with chocolate anthers; tapered and pointed buds, dark, coriaceous leaves. Fragrant.

WIENER CHARME
('J. Korschaprat', 'Charme de Vienne', 'Charming Vienna', 'Vienne Charm') by R. Kordes, 1963. Parentage: 'Chantre' × 'Golden Sun'. Vigorous and erect; large corollas of 27 petals. Fragrant. Royal National Rose Society award, 1963.

WIENERWALD
('Vienne Woods') by Kordes, 1974. Parentage: 'Colour Wonder' × seed plant. Vigorous, upright, and bushy; large, double corollas, pink to orange, large, dark, coriaceous leaves. Fragrant.

White Prince

White Wings

Wiener Charme

Wienerwald

WIMI
('Tanrowisa') by M. Tantau, 1983. Parentage unknown. Bushy; large, well-formed corollas of 20 petals, brilliant pink with silver underside, ample, dark, slightly shiny leaves. Very fragrant.

WINI EDMUNDS
by Sam McGredy IV, 1973. Parentage: 'Red Lion' × 'Hanne'. Vigorous and erect; large, double corollas, red with white undersides, dark, coriaceous leaves. Fragrant.

YASAKA
by Keihan Hirakata Nursery, 1972. Parentage: 'Miss Ireland' × 'Polynesian Sunset'. Corollas of 50 petals, salmon-orange with white underside.

YELLOW GIANT
by Lammerts, 1970. Large corollas of 25–30 petals, yellow flushed apricot. Fruit fragrance.

Wimi

Yasaka

Wini Edmunds

Yellow Giant

YOKO
by T. Shirakawa, 1981. Parentage: ('Happiness' ×
seedling) × 'Prominent'. Large corollas of 30–35 petals,
deep orange. Fragrant.

YOUKI-SAN
('Meidona', 'Mme. Neige') by Meilland, 1965. Parentage:
'Lady Sylvia' × 'White Knight'. Tall; large corollas of 40
petals, light green leaves. Very fragrant. Gold Medal Baden
Baden, 1964.

YU-AI
by S. Suzuki, 1970. Parentage: 'Sarabande' seed × 'Peace'
seed. Large corollas of 40–50 petals, cyclamen red.

YUGIRI
by S. Suzuki, 1987. Parentage: 'Pristine' × 'Seika'.
Corollas of 30 petals, white at the young stage then flushed
and edged vermilion-pink.

YUKO
by M. Isii, 1979. Parentage: sport of 'Bridal Pink'.
Corollas fuchsia-pink streaked white.

YUZEN
by S. Suzuki, 1982. Parentage: seed plant × 'Confidence'.
Classified among the Grandiflora. Erect; large, urn-shaped
corollas of 50 petals, pink edged dark red, dark, shiny
leaves, prickles turned downward.

YVES PIAGET
('Meivildo', 'Queen Adelaide') by M. L. Meilland, 1983.
Parentage: (('Pharoah' × 'Peace') × ('Chrysler Imperial'
× 'Charles Mallerin')) × 'Tamango'. Erect; large corollas
of more than 40 petals, dark, slightly shiny leaves. Very
fragrant.

ZAMBRA '80
('Meirilocra') by M. L. Meilland, 1979. Parentage: seed
plant × 'Banzai'. Greenhouse variety: large corollas of 35
petals, dark, opaque leaves. Slight fragrance.

Yoko

Youki-San

Yugiri

Yu-ai

Yuko

Yves Piaget

Yuzen

Zambra '80

Floribunda Roses

Polyantha Roses and Floribunda Roses

Matching strides with the Tea Hybrids during the 20th century are roses with an even more complex origin that have been classified, after some uncertainty and confusion, as Floribunda; that is, rose shrubs with corymbed flowers.

By and large, these are not "show" roses, although there are some exceptions. Still, at times their flowers are so similar (but smaller) to those of the Tea Hybrids as to give rise to differing opinions regarding in which group they belong. These are generally "chorus" roses, destined for cultivation in groups, bunches, and hedges, and for filling in and providing color and cheer. This is not to diminish their worth and relegate them to an inferior category. The Floribunda may even be more pleasing than the majestic Tea Hybrids, and they possess a pedigree that reveals all the nobility of their origins, even though they were often the result of chance hybridizations rather than exhaustive research.

In order to arrive at this type of rose, whose most dazzling virtue is its highly floriferous quality, we must take a step backward and become acquainted with the *Rosa multiflora* or *Rosa polyantha*. These roses, originating in East Asia, were climbers that produced cream-white panicles of flowers, similar to those of a bramble, and were introduced in Europe in 1862.

In the Lyon nursery of Guillot, the creator of 'La France', a *Rosa multiflora* spontaneously cross-fertilized itself with a Chinese dwarf, the 'Dwarf Pink China'. The result was two shrubs only some eight inches tall, 'Paquêrette' and 'Mignonette', the first and never-to-be-forgotten roses from a small group that maintained its place in history under the name Polypom. During the Victorian age some of these were very much loved: 'White Pet' (1879), the golden 'Perle d'Or', and, in particular, the luminous 'Cécile Brunner' (1881), of which a climbing form was discovered in America.

As the parents of the Polypoms were several (which is often the case with other classes of roses), one can find a bit of everything in this group: different sizes, different corolla shapes, different growth and vegetative development. But in the 20th century a group was identified as having enough characteristics in common to justify the creation of a new classification. Thus were born the Polyantha dwarfs, with their bunches of small and double flowers appearing as so many little tufts. These are truly charming and beautiful roses which are ideal for forming pretty groups on lawns. They are very short, highly adaptable, quite healthy and, most importantly, very resistent to intense cold. Nearly two hundred varieties were created during the first twenty years of this century, but many were nothing more than spontaneous mutations of such roses as 'Superb' and 'Orléans Rose'. In fact we know of twenty-nine mutations of this latter rose alone.

Arriving on the scene around 1920 to give impetus and new blood was the Dane Dines Poulsen. After several attempts she crossed the 'Orléans Rose' with a Tea Rose Hybrid and obtained the 'Else Poulsen' and 'Kirsten Poulsen'. These roses were the first in a long series that bore the family last name. 'Rumba' from 1958 and 'Hakuun' from 1962—the names have at this point become quite exotic—show how the production of the Poulsen firm has weathered the years.

Hybridization work between Polyantha and Tea Hybrids continued for some ten years. The number of varieties increased sufficiently to warrant a different class again, and thereby acquiring the right to a new name: Polyantha Hybrids. The previous dwarf Polyantha was slowly but inexorably replaced by these more recent hybrids which, after numerous cross-fertilizations, had obtained larger corollas as well as greater height. Several Polyanthas managed to avoid the massacre, notably several cultivars by de Ruiter including the older 'Gloria Mundi' and 'Cameo', as well as more recent cultivars such as the bronze-leafed 'Rosemary Rose'. Also winning the race against time was 'The Fairy', by Ann

Bentall, which dates to 1932 and is still much in evidence.

By around 1940 these new hybrids were securely established in gardens. They had become the fierce rivals of the Tea Hybrids, though having a very different function; their color range, originally limited to red and pink, had become quite vast, with single shapes and double forms, and a fragrance had also returned. In order to confer greater dignity on this emerging class, botanists felt they had to change its name yet again, and the Floribunda and Floribunda Hybrids were born, listed in the catalogues as Perpetual Roses with flower clusters.

Standing out at first in the production of the Floribunda, beside Poulsen, was Edward Le Grice. In 1940 he had already presented rose-lovers with the unbeatable 'Dainty Maid', and in 1946 the 'Dusky Maiden', which was even more fragrant. Assisted by Peter Beales, a future author and rose cultivator of importance, Le Grice experimented with new crosses using different parents, even the *Rosa gallica*. His successes include 'Lilac Charm', and 'Allgold', his pride and joy, which received an award in London, as did many of his creations.

The Americans Lammerts and Boerner worked tirelessly for the firm Jackson & Perkins. These gentlemen put their signatures on: 'Goldilocks'; the multi-award-winning 'Fashion'; 'Masquerade'; the delightful 'Apricot Nectar'; the fragrant 'Saratoga'; and the virginal 'White Bouquet'. Boerner specialized particularly in double-flowered Floribunda. Also of note are the Floribundas of Herbert Swim, who introduced us to 'Circus', 'County Fair', and 'Moonsprite', winner of two gold medals.

Hybridizers busily experimented, selecting, cultivated, and spread the Floribunda Roses. In the middle of his work on Tea Hybrids, Pat Dickson stuck in some ten Floribunda; 'Princess Michiko' deserves mention here. Sam McGredy IV created twenty-four Floribunda, including 'City of Leeds', 'Irish Mist', and 'Picasso', called "hand painted", as some particularly artistic roses are described.

Meilland has given us a host of Floribunda: 'Cocoricò', gold-medal-winner at Genoa and London; 'Sarabande', which triumphs on lawns around the world and gained maximum recognition in all the competitions in 1957, including Bagatelle, Geneva, Rome, Portland, and All-America Rose Selections; 'Zambra', incandescent as glowing embers and gold-medal-winner at Rome; 'Kalinka', as delightful as its name and winner of the gold medal at Madrid and Belfast; 'Rusticana', given an award at Geneva and Rome; and 'Charleston'.

A careful and productive hybridizer such as Kordes could not miss out on the show, and we have: 'Pinocchio' (1940), whose parents are a *moschata*, a Tea, and a Polyantha, a mixture that turned out to be excellent; and 'Orange Triumph'. We owe to his son Reimer, however, the greatest and most long-lasting success of all time, 'Schneewittchen', or 'Iceberg', given an award at Baden Baden and London. Also from Reimer 'Lilli Marlene', the Gold Rose at The Hague, and 'Friesia', gold-medal-winner at Baden Baden.

Though the Japanese came on the scene a little later, by 1980 their production of Floribunda had become immense and of high quality. Suzuki has given us a good number through the Keisei Nurseries of Tokyo. Their names may be difficult for us, but the roses are charming: 'Hanagasumi', soft-white in color; 'Hanabusa', which derives from 'Sarabande'; 'Hanagasa', vermilion and fragrant; 'Ko-Choh', bicolored and fragrant. 'Tchin-Tchin' might seem to be Japanese but comes from Antibes, created by Paolino of the Meilland family.

During the 1980s the Floribunda came to us by way of famous hybridizers and firms: 'Tequila', once again by Meilland (1982); 'Gartenzauber' by Kordes (1984); 'Amber Queen' by Harkness; and the 1987 Rose of the Year, 'La Paloma' by Tantau (1985); 'Lady Romsay' by Peter Beales (1985); and 'Ards Beauty' and 'Wishing' by Dickson (1986). New names asserted themselves, among them the American Warriner, who presented the coral-colored 'Cherish' which received an award at the All America Rose Selections, and 'Sun Flare' which received awards in both America and Japan.

The Floribunda, which are coral roses, are not expected to triumph because of the radiant beauty of the individual flower, but rather to make an impression by their overall effect. This effect is guaranteed by their first-rate reflowering. These qualities have made the Floribunda a precious decorative element wherever a note of vivid color is required on lawns, in mixed borders of gardens, on terraces and balconies, and even in corporate and urban green areas. Their many uses, their exuberance, and their liveliness assure a continued demand for Floribunda, and thus their continued production; the number of cultivars is already in the thousands.

Precisely because they are so profuse, types are grouped for similarity in height (though in general they are below thirty-five inches), vegetative growth, quality, and design of the flowers. Some are similar to those of a Polyantha, some bring to mind the Tea Roses while others are simple. Thus, the tendency of certain authors and official organizations—Americans more than others—to classify various Floribundas with particularly large corollas under the name of Grandiflora Rose is justified.

ANNE-MARIE DE MONTRAVEL
(*'Anna-Maria de Montravel'*) *by Rambaux, 1879.*
Parentage: a multiflora rose with double flowers × *'Mme. de Tartas'. Dwarf, compact; small corollas in clusters even of 60 flowers, double, irregularly-shaped when open, pure white, glossy leaves, dark on the upper side, silvery on the underside, thin prickles. Lily of the valley fragrance.*

BABY BETTY
by Burbage Nursery, 1929. Parentage: 'Eblouissant' × *'Comtesse du Cayla'. Small corollas, pink on soft pink base.*

BABY FAURAX
by L. Lille, 1924. Dwarf; small, double corollas in large clusters. Fragrant.

BRITANNIA
by Burbage Nursery, 1929. Parentage: 'Coral Cluster' × *'Eblouissant'. Corollas of 5 petals in groups of 10–40 flowers, scarlet pink on a white base. Fragrant.*

Baby Betty

Baby Faurax

Anne-Marie de Montravel

Britannia

Cécile Brünner

Fireglow

Maréchal Foch

CÉCILE BRÜNNER
('Mignon', 'Mlle. Cécile Brünner', 'Mme. Cécile Brünner', 'Sweetheart Rose') by V.ve Ducher, 1881. Parentage: a double-flowered Multiflora rose × 'Souvenir d'un Ami'. Dwarf, with similar growth as a Tea.

FIREGLOW
by Wezelenburg, 1929. Parentage: sport of 'Orange King'. Dwarf, compact; semidouble corollas, vermilion flushed orange. Slight fragrance.

MARÉCHAL FOCH
by L. Vasseur, 1918. Parentage: sport of 'Orléans Rose'.

MIGNONETTE
by Guillot Fils, 1880. Parentage: a double-flowered Multiflora Rose × probably a Chinese Rose or a Tea. Very dwarf, bushy; small, double corollas in short panicles of 50 flowers, pink at times almost white and bordered by wine-red spots.

Mignonette

ORANGE TRIUMPH
by Kordes, 1937. Parentage: 'Eva' × 'Solarium'. Compact, bushy; small, semidouble, cup-shaped corollas, glossy leaves.

PERLE D'OR
('Yellow Cecile Brunner') by Rambaux, 1884. Parentage: a Polyantha × 'Mme. Falcot'. Nearly one yard tall; very double corollas, golden pink, soft, deep green leaves.

THE FAIRY
by A. Bentall, 1932. Parentage: 'Paul Crampel' × 'Lady Gay'. Compact, wide growth, cold resistant, perennial; small, double corollas, minute, glossy leaves.

TRAVEMÜNDE
by Kordes, 1968. Parentage: 'Lilli Marleen' × 'Ama'. Medium, double corollas, ovoid buds, dark leaves.

YOROKOBI
by S. Suzuki, 1955. Small, single, double and semidouble corollas, white, pink, or red.

The Fairy

Travemünde

Orange Triumph

Perle d'Or

Yorokobi

Akemi

Akito

Allgold

Amanogawa

America's Junior Miss

Amsterdam

Anabell

Angel Face

AKEMI
by Keisei Rose Nursery, 1977. Parentage: ('Sarabande' × 'Hawaii') × ('Sarabande' × 'Ruby Lips'). Vigorous and erect; medium corollas, cup-shaped, of 33 petals, dark leaves. Slight fragrance.

AKITO
('Tanito') by Tantau, 1974. Parentage: 'Zorina' × 'Nordia'. Erect and bushy; medium corollas, ovoid buds, medium green leaves. Slight fragrance.

ALLGOLD
by Le Grice, 1956. Parentage: 'Goldilocks' × 'Ellinor Le Grice'. Vigorous; large corollas of 15–22 petals, solitary and in large bunches, small, dark, and shiny leaves. Slight fragrance. Gold Medal Royal National Rose Society, 1956.

AMANOGAWA
by S. Suzuki, 1956. Parentage: 'Golden Scepter' seed × seedling. Single corollas, deep yellow.

AMERICA'S JUNIOR MISS
by Boerner, 1964. Parentage: 'Seventeen' × 'Demure' from seed. Vigorous, bushy; medium corollas, double, coral-pink, shiny leaves. Fragrant.

AMSTERDAM
('Havam') by T. Verschuren, 1972. Parentage: 'Europeana' × 'Parkdirektor Riggers'. Vigorous; large, semidouble corollas of 12–15 petals, geranium-red, ovoid buds, shiny, reddish brown leaves. Gold Medal The Hague, 1972.

ANABELL
('Korbell') by Kordes, 1972. Parentage: 'Zorina' × 'Colour Wonder'. Large, well-formed corollas of 30 petals, orange shaded silver, small leaves. Fragrant.

ANGEL FACE
by Swim & Weeks, 1968. Parentage: ('Circus' × 'Lavender Pinocchio') × 'Sterling Silver'. Vigorous, erect, bushy; large, undulating corollas of 30 petals, from mauve to lavender, dark, coriaceous, and shiny leaves. Very fragrant. Prize All-America Rose Selections, 1969, American Rose Society, 1971.

Baby Blaze

Bellona

Belinda

APRICOT NECTAR
by Boerner, 1965. Parentage: seed plant × 'Spartan'.
Vigorous, bushy; large corollas, cup-shaped and double,
apricot pink on a gold base, dark and shiny leaves. Strong,
fruity fragrance. Prize All-America Rose Selections, 1966.

BABY BLAZE
('Lund's Jubiläum') by W. Kordes, 1954. Parentage:
'World's Fair' × 'Hamburg'. Vigorous, bushy, and compact;
large corollas, semi-cup-shaped, cherry with white eyes, light,
shiny leaves. Fragrant.

BELINDA
('Tanbeedee') by Tantau, 1971. Parentage: seed plant ×
'Zorina'. Vigorous, erect, and bushy; medium, double
corollas, from bronze to orange, ovoid buds. Fragrant.

BELLONA
('Korilona') by R. Kordes, 1976. Parentage: 'New Day' ×
'Minigold'. Very vigorous, erect; large corollas of 27 petals,
pointed, ovoid buds, light leaves. Lightly fragrant.

Apricot Nectar

Bridal Pink

Chacok

Betty Prior

Charisma

Castanet

BETTY PRIOR
by Prior, 1935. Parentage: 'Kristen Poulsen' × unnamed
seed plant. Vigorous, bushy; single corollas, cupped,
carmine-pink, ovoid buds. Very floriferous. Strong, spicy
fragrance. Gold Medal Royal National Rose Society, 1935.

BRIDAL PINK
by Boerner, 1967. Parentage: 'Summertime' from seed ×
'Spartan' from seed. Graft variety. Vigorous, erect, and
bushy; turbinate corollas, large and double, ovoid, pointed
buds, coriaceous leaves.

Cherish

Class Act

Charleston

CASTANET
by Boerner, 1960. Parentage: 'Chic' × 'Garnette' from seed. Erect, bushy; large corollas of 45 petals, orange-pink with lighter undersides, ovoid buds. Fragrant.

CHACOK
('Pigalle', 'Meicloux', 'Jubilee 150') by M. L. Meilland, 1983. Parentage: 'Frenzy' × (('Sambra' × 'Suspense') × 'King's Ransom')). Bushy; large corollas of 40 petals, yellow suffused with orange and red, medium green leaves, semiglossy. No fragrance.

CHARISMA
by E. G. Hill Co., 1977. Parentage: 'Gemini' × 'Zorina'. Vigorous, erect, bushy; medium corollas of 40 petals, turbinate, scarlet and yellow, shiny, coriaceous leaves. Slightly fragrant.

CHARLESTON
('Meiridge') by A. Meilland, 1963. Parentage: 'Masquerade' × ('Radar' × 'Caprice'). Erect, compact; large corollas of 20 petals, yellow suffused with crimson and ending in crimson, pointed buds, dark, coriaceous, shiny leaves.

CHERISH
('Jacsal') by Warriner, 1980. Parentage: 'Bridal Pink' × 'Matador'. Compact with wide growth; large corollas of 28 petals, turbinate, coral-pink, short buds, wide, dark leaves. Slightly fragrant. All-America Rose Selections award, 1980.

CLASS ACT
by Warriner, 1988. Parentage: 'Sun Flare' × unnamed seedling. Vigorous and disease resistant; semidouble corollas in large bunches, white, dark green, glossy leaves. All-America Rose Selections, 1989.

Circus

Concertino

City of Leeds

Dr. Faust

Cocorico

County Fair

Dusky Maiden

E-higasa

CIRCUS
by Swim, 1956. Parentage: 'Fandango' × 'Pinocchio'. Bushy; large corollas of 52 petals in large bunches, yellow marked with pink, salmon, or scarlet; semiglossy, coriaceous leaves. Fragrance with scent between tea and spice. Gold Medal Geneva and Royal National Rose Society, 1955, All-America Rose Selections, 1956.

CITY OF LEEDS
by S. McGredy IV, 1966. Parentage: 'Evelyn Fison' × ('Spartan' × 'Red Favorite'). Large corollas of 19 petals, dark leaves. Slightly fragrant. Gold Medal Royal National Rose Society, 1965.

COCORICO
by F. Meilland, 1951. Parentage: 'Alain' × 'Orange Triumph'. Vigorous, erect, bushy; large, single corollas of 5 petals, shiny and brilliant leaves. Spicy fragrance. Gold Medal Geneva and Royal National Rose Society, 1951.

CONCERTINO
('Meibinosor') by M. L. Meilland, 1976. Parentage: (('Fidelio' × 'Fidelio') × ('Zambra' × 'Zambra')) × 'Marlena'. Vigorous, compact; medium corollas of 20 petals, flat up to the cup, dark, opaque leaves. Slightly fragrant.

COUNTY FAIR
by Swim, 1960. Parentage: 'Frolic' × 'Pink Bountiful'. Vigorous, compact; large, flat corollas of 8–10 petals, medium to dark pink, pointed buds, coriaceous, dark, semiglossy leaves. Slight fragrance.

DR. FAUST
('Faust'), by R. Kordes, 1957. Parentage: 'Masquerade' × 'Golden Scepter'. Vigorous, bushy; medium corollas of 25 petals in large bunches, yellow gold shaded orange pink, dark, shiny leaves. Fragrant. Gold Medal Royal National Rose Society, 1956.

DUSKY MAIDEN
by Le Grice, 1947. Parentage: ('Daily Mail Scented Rose' × 'Étoile de Hollande') × 'Else Poulsen'. Vigorous; large, single corollas, dark leaves. Fragrant. Gold Medal Royal National Rose Society, 1948.

E-HIGASA
by Keihan Hirakata Nursery, 1974. Parentage: 'Masquerade' × 'Lydia'. Double corollas of 30–35 petals, red on a yellow base.

ESTHER OFARIM
('Matador') by R. Kordes, 1972. Parentage: 'Colour Wonder' × 'Zorina'. Classified among the Hybrid Tea Roses. Vigorous; medium, double corollas, turbinate, scarlet to orange, large leaves, dark, coriaceous. Fragrant.

EUROPEANA
by De Ruiter, 1963. Parentage: 'Ruth Leuwerik' × 'Rosemary Rose'. Vigorous; large, double corollas in rosette shape in thick bunches, bronze-green leaves. Slight fragrance. Gold Medal The Hague, 1962, All-American Rose Selections award, 1968.

FABERGÉ
by Boerner, 1969. Parentage: seed plant × 'Zorina'. Vigorous, thick, and bushy; large, double corollas, peach-pink with yellowish undersides, dark, coriaceous leaves. Slight fragrance.

FASHION
by Boerner, 1949. Parentage: 'Pinocchio' × 'Crimson Glory'. Vigorous, bushy; large corollas of 23 petals, bright coral-pink, ovoid buds, dark peach pink. Fragrant. Gold Medal Royal National Rose Society, 1948, Bagatelle and Portland, 1949, All-America Rose Selections award and Gold Medal American Rose Society, 1954.

FIDELIO
('Meichest') by Alain Meilland, 1964. Parentage: ('Radar' × 'Caprice') × 'Fire King'. Erect, vigorous; medium corollas of 35 petals, tapered and pointed buds, coriaceous leaves. Slight fragrance.

FINALE
by R. Kordes, 1964. Parentage: 'Nordlicht' × 'Meteor'.

FLAMBÉE
by Mallerin, 1954. Medium-large corollas of 25–30 petals, flaming red.

FLORADORA
by Tantau, 1944. Parentage: 'Baby Chateau' × Rosa roxburghii. Erect, bushy; medium corollas of 25 petals, cup-shaped, cinnabar red, globular buds, coriaceous, shiny leaves. Fragrant. All-America Rose Selections award, 1945.

FLORIAN
('Tender Night', 'Meilaur') by Meilland, 1971. Parentage: 'Tamango' × ('Fire King' × 'Banzai'). Erect; large corollas of 25 petals, dark, opaque leaves. Slight, fruity fragrance. Gold Medal Rome, 1971.

Esther Ofarim

Europeana

Fabergé

Fashion

Flambée

Fidelio

Floradora

Finale

Florian

FLORIDOR

by Delbard, 1974. Well-formed corollas, deep orange.

FLOWER GIRL

('Sea Pearl') by P. Dickson, 1964. Parentage: 'Kordes' Perfecta' × 'Montezuma'. Erect and bushy; well-formed corollas of 24 petals, large, delicate pink with undersides suffused with peach and yellow, long, pointed buds, dark leaves.

FRENCH LACE

('Jaclace') by W. A. Warriner, 1981. Parentage: 'Dr. A. J. Verhage' × 'Bridal Pink'. Bushy; corollas of 30 petals, apricot-ivory and white, pointed buds, small, dark leaves, tiny prickles. Barely fragrant. All-America Rose Selections award, 1982.

FRENSHAM

by Norman, 1946. Parentage: Floribunda seed plant × 'Crimson Glory'. Vigorous; medium and semidouble corollas of 15 petals. Slight fragrance. Gold Medal Royal National Rose Society, 1943, and American Rose Society, 1955.

FRIESIA

('Sunsprite', 'Korresia') by R. Kordes, 1977. Parentage: seed plant × 'Spanish Sun'. Erect; large corollas, flat, with 28 petals, light leaves. Very fragrant. Gold Medal Baden Baden, 1972.

FRUITÉ

by Meilland, 1985. Double corollas of 25 petals, scarlet-orange on a yellow base and underside.

GABRIELLA

('Bergme') by Berggren, 1977. Vigorous, bushy; large corollas, cup-shaped, of 33 petals, ovoid buds, shiny leaves. Slight fragrance.

GARNETTE

by Tantau, 1951. Parentage: ('Rosenelfe' × 'Eva') × 'Eros'. Greenhouse variety, bushy; small corollas of 50 petals, red on a base of lemon-yellow, dark, coriaceous leaves. Slight fragrance.

GARTENZAUBER '84

('Gartenzauber', 'Kornacho') by W. Kordes, 1984. Parentage: (seed plant × 'Tornado') × 'Chorus'. Erect; large corollas of 35 petals, dark, semiglossy leaves. Slight fragrance.

Floridor

Flower Girl

French Lace

Frensham

Gabriella

Friesia

Garnette

Fruité

Gartenzauber '84

Gene Boerner

Ginger

Glacier

Golden Slippers

GENE BOERNER
by Boerner, 1968. Parentage: 'Ginger' × ('Ma Perkins' × 'Garnette Supreme'). Vigorous and erect; medium corollas of 35 petals, ovoid buds, shiny leaves.

GINGER
by Boerner, 1962. Parentage: 'Garnette' from seed × 'Spartan'. Vigorous, compact, and bushy; large corollas, cup-shaped, of 28 petals, in irregular bunches, ovoid buds, coriaceous leaves. Fragrant.

GLACIER
by Boerner, 1952. Parentage: hybrid of unrecorded white Tea Rose × 'Summer Snow'. Vigorous, erect; large corollas, cup-shaped, of 28 petals, white with yellow shadows, dark, shiny leaves. Fragrant.

GOLD BUNNY
('Gold Badge', 'Meigronuri') by Paolino, 1978. Parentage: 'Poppy Flash' × ('Charleston' × 'Allgold'). Vigorous; large corollas, cup shaped, of 38 petals, conical buds.

GOLDEN SLIPPERS
by Von Abrams, 1961. Parentage: 'Goldilocks' × seed plant. Vigorous, compact, low; large corollas of 23 petals, turbinate, yellow suffused with vermilion with golden centers, pointed buds, coriaceous, shiny leaves. Fragrant. Gold Medal Portland, 1960, All-America Rose Selections award, 1962.

Gold Bunny

Golden Treasure

Great News

Green Fire

GOLDEN TREASURE
('Goldschatz') by M. Tantau, 1964. Erect and bushy; large, double corollas, pointed buds, dark, shiny leaves.

GREAT NEWS
by Le Grice, 1973. Parentage: 'Rose Gaujard' × 'City of Hereford'. Moderate growth; large corollas of 33 petals, prune with silver undersides, thick leaves of olive-green. Very fragrant.

GREEN FIRE
by Swim, 1958. Parentage: 'Goldilocks' × seed plant. Vigorous, bushy; large, flat, semidouble corollas of 13 petals, ovoid, pointed buds, semiglossy leaves. Slight fragrance.

HAKUUN
by N. D. Poulsen, 1962. Parentage: seed plant × ('Pinocchio' × 'Pinocchio'). Compact, bushy, low; medium, semidouble corollas of 15 petals, cream-white, small buds, clear green leaves. Slight fragrance.

HAMBURG'S LOVE
by Timmermans Roses, 1974. Parentage: 'Fragrant Cloud' × 'Manx Queen'. Compact; large corollas of 28 petals, shiny leaves. Very fragrant.

HANA-BUSA
by S. Suzuki, 1981. Parentage: 'Sarabande' × ('Rumba' × 'Olympic Torch'). Bushy; medium, flat, semidouble corollas of 18 petals, ovoid buds, straight prickles.

HANAGASA
by Suzuki, 1968. Parentage: ('Hawaii' × seed plant) × 'Miss Ireland'. Vigorous; large corollas, cup shaped, of 23 petals, globular buds, large, clear green leaves. Fragrant.

HANA-GASUMI
by S. Suzuki, 1985. Parentage: 'Europeana' × ('Myo-joh' × 'Fidelio'). Bushy; medium, semidouble, flat corollas of 13 petals, white then maturing to pink; dark, semiglossy leaves, small, hook-shaped prickles turned downward. Fragrant.

HANAKAGO
by S. Suzuki, 1972. Parentage: 'Sarabande' from seed × 'Rondo' from seed. Double corollas of 30–40 petals, vermilion.

Hakuun

Hanagasa

Hamburg's Love

Hana-Gasumi

Hana-Busa

Hanakago

Happy Event

Heinz Erhardt

Heat Wave

Holstein

Iceberg

Ingrid Weibull

Intrigue

Irish Mist

A HAPPY EVENT
by P. Dickson, 1974. Parentage: ('Karl Herbst' × 'Masquerade') × 'Rose Gaujard'. Moderate growth; large semidouble corollas of 12 petals, pale chrome yellow suffused with pink, shiny leaves.

HEAT WAVE
('Mme. Paula Guisez') by Swim, 1958. Parentage: seed plant × 'Roundelay'. Vigorous, erect, bushy; large corollas, cup-shaped, of 30 petals, urn-shaped buds, rounded, dark, semiglossy leaves. Slight fragrance.

HEINZ ERHARDT
by R. Kordes, 1962. Vigorous, bushy; large corollas of 25 petals, bronze leaves. Slight fragrance. Gold Medal Baden Baden, 1961.

HOLSTEIN
('Firefly') by Kordes, 1939. Parentage: 'Else Poulsen' × 'Dance of Joy' from seed. Very vigorous, bushy; large, cup-shaped, simple corollas of 6 petals in immense bunches, pointed buds, dark, coriaceous, bronze leaves. Slight fragrance. Gold Medal Portland, 1939.

ICEBERG
('Korbin', 'Schneewittchen', 'Fée des Neiges') by R. Kordes, 1958. Parentage: 'Robin Hood' × 'Virgo'. Vigorous, erect, bushy; double corollas, pure white, tapered and pointed buds, light green, shiny leaves. Very fragrant. Gold Medal Royal National Rose Society, 1958, Certificate of Merit Rose Horticultural Society, 1961, Gold Medal Baden Baden, 1958.

INGRID WEIBULL
('Showbiz', 'Tanweike', 'Bernhard Daneke Rose') by M. Tantau, 1981. Parentage unknown. Bushy; medium corollas of 20 petals, dark, semiglossy leaves. No fragrance. All-America Rose Selections award, 1985.

INTRIGUE
('Jacum') by Warriner, 1984. Parentage: 'White Masterpiece' × 'Heirloom'. Large corollas of 20 petals, dark, semiglossy leaves. Very fragrant. All-America Rose Selections award, 1984.

IRISH MIST
by S. McGredy IV, 1966. Parentage: 'Orangeade' × 'Mischief'. Very bushy; large, well-formed corollas, salmon-orange, dark leaves. Slight fragrance.

JACK FROST
by R. G. Jelly, 1962. Parentage: 'Garnette' × seed plant. Greenhouse variety, erect and vigorous; medium corollas of 42 petals, from white to cream, pointed buds, dark leaves. Fragrant.

JAN SPEK
by S. McGredy IV, 1966. Parentage: 'Cläre Grammerstorf' × 'Faust'. Large, flat corollas of 44 petals, dark and shiny leaves. Slight fragrance. Gold Medal Belfast, 1968, and The Hague, 1970.

JELCANODIR
by R. G. Jelly, 1976. Parentage: Unknown × 'Golden Garnette'. Medium corollas of 25–30 petals, yellow.

JOFITALI
by De Witte, 1976. Parentage: sport of 'Sonia'. Pink corollas with cardinal red centers.

KALINKA
('Pink Wonder', 'Meihartflor') by Meilland, 1970. Parentage: 'Zambra × ('Sarabande' × ('Goldilocks' × 'Fashion')). Vigorous and erect; large corollas of 28 petals, imbricate, shiny, coriaceous leaves. Very fragrant. Gold Medal Madrid, 1969, and Belfast, 1972.

KO-CHOH
by S. Suzuki, 1983. Parentage: ('Rumba' × 'Olympic Torch') × 'Allgold'. Compact, low; small corollas of 45 petals in small bunches, orange with underside of yellow suffused with orange, dark, semiglossy leaves, tiny prickles. Fragrant.

KŌRIN
by S. Suzuki, 1988. Parentage: 'Ambassador' × 'Gold Bunny'. Large, double corollas, deep apricot or bright orange.

KORONA
('Kornita') by Kordes, 1955. Vigorous, erect; medium corollas of 20 petals. Slight fragrance. Gold Medal Royal National Rose Society, 1954.

Jack Frost

Jan Spek

Jelcanodir

Jofitali

Kōrin

Kalinka

Ko-Choh

Korona

La Sevillana

Lavaglut

Lilibet

Lilli Marleen

Little Darling

LA SEVILLANA

('Meigekanu') by M. L. Meilland, 1978. Parentage: (('Meibrim' × 'Jolie Madame') × ('Zambra' × 'Zambra')) × (('Tropicana' × 'Tropicana') × ('Poppy Flash' × 'Rusticana')). Vigorous, bushy; medium, semidouble corollas of 13 petals, conical buds, bronze leaves.

LAVAGLUT

('Korlech', 'Intrigue', 'Lavaglow') by W. Kordes' Sohne, 1978. Parentage: 'Bruss an Bayern' × seed plant. Vigorous, erect, bushy; medium, globular corollas of 24 petals, shiny leaves. Slight fragrance.

LILIBET

('Fairy Princess') by Lindquist, 1953. Parentage: 'Floradora' × 'Pinocchio'. Bushy, low; large corollas with 30 petals, ovoid buds, shiny leaves. Spicy fragrance.

LILLI MARLEEN

('Korlima') by R. Kordes, 1959. Parentage: ('Our Princess' × 'Rudolph Timm') × 'Ama'. Vigorous; large, cup-shaped corollas of 25 petals, ovoid buds, coriaceous leaves. Fragrant. Gold Medal Royal National Rose Society, 1959, Certificate of Merit Royal Horticultural Society, 1959, Golden Rose at The Hague, 1966.

LITTLE DARLING

by Duehrsen, 1956. Parentage: 'Capt. Thomas' × ('Baby Château' × 'Fashion'). Very vigorous, with wide growth; medium corollas of beautiful form with 27 petals, yellow and salmon pink, ovoid buds, dark, coriaceous, shiny leaves. Spicy fragrance. Gold Medal Portland, 1958, American Rose Society award, 1964.

MAGALI

by Meilland, 1986. Corollas of 30 petals, coral-pink.

MALIBU

by Morey, 1959. Parentage: 'Charlotte Armstrong' × 'Independence'. Corollas of 35 petals, coral.

MARINA

('Rinakor') by Kordes, 1974. Parentage: 'Colour Wonder' × seed plant. Vigorous and erect; double corollas, orange on a base of yellow, dark, shiny, coriaceous leaves. Fragrant. All-America Rose Selections award, 1981.

Magali

Malibu

Marina

MASQUERADE

by Boerner, 1949. Parentage: 'Goldilocks' × 'Holiday'.
Vigorous, bushy, compact; medium, semidouble corollas of
17 petals, brilliant yellow that turns to salmon-pink and
finally dark red, dark, coriaceous leaves. Slight fragrance.
Gold Medal Royal National Rose Society, 1952.

MAXIM

by Tantau, 1961. Medium corollas of 25 petals, vermilion.

MEINARGONIS

by Meilland, 1981. Vigorous, bushy; medium corollas, ruby
red.

MEIROLADELL

by Meilland. Parentage: (seedling × 'Zorina') × (seedling
× seedling). Double corollas, vermilion-orange.

MEITOFLAPO

by M. L. Meilland, 1980. Parentage: ('Jack Frost' ×
('Zambra' × ('Baccara' × 'White Knight'))) ×
(('Zambra' × ('Baccará' × 'White Knight')) × seed
plant). Greenhouse variety; large corollas of 29 petals,
small, dark, semiglossy leaves. No fragrance.

MEPHISTO

by Mallerin, 1951. Parentage: 'Français' × seedling.
Medium-large corollas, vermilion.

MIMI ROSE

('Mimi Pink', 'Jeldaniran') by R. G. Jelly, 1980.
Parentage: seed plant × 'Misty Pink'. Erect; grafting
variety; large corollas of 35 petals, pale pink with darker
undersides, dark, semiglossy leaves. No fragrance.

MIMOLLET

by Ota, 1975. Parentage: ('Queen Elizabeth' × 'Ethel
Sanday') × 'Zambra'. Erect; large corollas of 40 petals,
brilliant pink, shiny leaves.

MINUETTE

('Laminuette') by Lammerts, 1969. Parentage: 'Peace' ×
'Rumba'. Vigorous, bushy; medium, double corollas, ivory
edged in red, ovoid buds, dark, shiny leaves. Slight fragrance.

Masquerade

Maxim

Meinargonis

Meiroladell

Mimi Rose

Meitoflapo

Mimollet

Mephisto

Minuette

Mitzi '81

Nearly Wild

Mona Lisa

Montana

MITZI '81
by Meilland, 1981. Corollas of 25 petals, deep yellow.

MONA LISA
('Kormat', 'Australian Gold') by Kordes, 1980. Bushy; corollas of 20 petals in bunches of 5, ovoid buds, dark, coriaceous leaves, red prickles. Slightly fragrant.

MONTANA
('Royal Occasion') by Tantau, 1974. Parentage: 'Walzertraum' × 'Europeana'. Erect; large corollas of 20 petals, tapered and pointed buds, shiny leaves. Slightly fragrant.

MOONSPRITE
by Swim, 1956. Parentage: 'Sutter's Gold' × 'Ondine'. Dwarf, bushy; medium corollas, cup-shaped, of 80 petals, cream-white with pale gold center, coriaceous, semiglossy leaves. Very fragrant. Gold Medal Baden Baden, 1955, and Rome, 1956.

NEARLY WILD
by Brownell, 1941. Parentage: 'Dr. W. Fan Fleet' × 'Leuchstern'. Bushy; single corollas of 5 petals, small, tapered and pointed buds. Fragrant.

Moonsprite

News

Orange Bunny

Nicole

Paddy McGredy

Nishiki-e

Panorama Holiday

Papillon Rose

Parador

Patricia

NEWS
('Legnews') by Le Grice, 1968. Parentage: 'Lilac Charm' × 'Tuscany Superb'. Semidouble corollas, shiny, olive-green leaves. Gold Medal Royal National Rose Society, 1970.

NICOLE
('Korikole') by W. Kordes, 1984. Parentage: seed plant × 'Bordure Rose'. Erect; large corollas of 35 petals, white edged in pink, dark, semiglossy leaves. Slightly fragrant.

NISHIKI-E
by S. Suzuki, 1981. Parentage: ('Sarabande' × 'Amanogawa') × 'Kagayaki'. Erect; medium corollas of 38 petals, yellow-orange in small bunches, dark, semiglossy leaves, small prickles turned downward.

ORANGE BUNNY
('Meirianopur') by M. L. Meilland, 1959. Parentage: 'Scherzo' × ('Sarabande' × 'Frenzy'). Bushy; semidouble corollas of 13 petals, cup-shaped, red-orange with darker undersides, pointed buds, bronze, opaque, and very thick leaves.

PADDY MCGREDY
('Macpa') by S. McGredy IV, 1962. Parentage: 'Spartan' × 'Tzigane'. Vigorous, bushy; large corollas, cup-shaped, of 33 petals, ovoid buds, coriaceous leaves. Fragrant. Gold Medal Royal National Rose Society, 1961.

PANORAMA HOLIDAY
by Gregory, 1963. Parentage: 'Queen Elizabeth' × seed plant. Large corollas of 34 petals, pointed buds, dark, shiny leaves. Fragrant.

PAPILLON ROSE
by Lens, 1956. Parentage: 'White Briarcliff' × ('Lady Sylvia' × 'Fashion'). Vigorous, bushy; double corollas, pink suffused with salmon. Very fragrant.

PARADOR
('Meichanso') by Paolino, 1978. Parentage: (('Sarabande' × 'Meikim') × ('Alain' × 'Orange Triumph')) × 'Diablotin'. Very vigorous; large corollas of 20 petals, cup-shaped. Gold Medal Tokyo, 1978.

PATRICIA
('Korpatri') by Kordes, 1972. Parentage: sport of 'Elizabeth of Glamis'. Apricot corollas on a base suffused with gold. Gold Medal Orleans, 1979.

PERMANENT WAVE

('Duchess of Windsor', 'L'Indefrisible', 'Mevrouw von Straaten van Nes', 'Mrs. Van Nes', 'Van Nes') by M. Leenders, 1932. Parentage: sport of 'Else Poulsen'. Vigorous, bushy; large, semidouble corollas in big bunches, wavy petals, dark, shiny leaves. Slightly fragrant. Gold Medal Bagatelle, 1933, Rome, 1934.

PICASSO

('Macpic') by S. McGredy IV, 1971. Parentage: 'Marlena' × ('Evelyn Fison' × ('Frulingsmorgen' × 'Orange Sweetheart')). Large, semidouble corollas of 18 petals, intense pink edged clear pink with eyes and undersides white, minute leaves. Gold Medal Belfast and New Zealand, 1973.

PIMLICO '81

('Meidujaran') by M. L. Meilland, 1980. Parentage: ('Tamango' × 'Fidelio') × ('Charleston' × 'Lilli Marleen'). Bushy; large corollas of 35 petals, large, dark, and shiny leaves. No fragrance. Gold Medal Belfast, 1983.

PINK CHIFFON

by Boerner, 1956. Parentage: 'Fashion' × 'Fantasia'. Vigorous, bushy; large corollas of 53 petals, from cup-shaped to flat, shiny leaves. Very fragrant.

PINK ROSETTE

by Krebs, 1948. Vigorous, dwarf, bushy; medium corollas of 50 petals, rosette-shaped and cup-shaped, small ovoid buds, dark coriaceous leaves. Slightly fragrant.

PINOCCHIO

('Rosenmarchen') by Kordes, 1940. Parentage: 'Eva' × 'Golden Rapture'. Vigorous, bushy; small corollas of 30 petals, cup-shaped, pink suffused with salmon with darker edges, coriaceous leaves. Fruity fragrance. Gold Medal Portland, 1942.

PITICA

by Royan, 1976. Parentage: sport of 'Sonia'. Pale pink corollas.

POLKA

by M. L. Meilland, 1959. Parentage: 'Moulin Rouge' × 'Fashion'. Vigorous, bushy; large corollas of 42 petals, turbinate and cup-shaped, flat at the top, coriaceous leaves. Fragrant.

Permanent Wave

Picasso

Pimlico '81

Pinocchio

Pink Chiffon

Pitica

Pink Rosette

Polka

Ponderosa

Princess Chichibu

Princess Michiko

Purple Splendor

Queen Silvia

PONDEROSA
('Korpon') by R. Kordes, 1970. Parentage: seed plant ×
'Marlena'. Dwarf, vigorous, bushy; medium corollas, double,
cup-shaped, globular buds, coriaceous leaves. Slightly
fragrant.

PRINCESS CHICHIBU
by Harkness, 1971. Parentage: ('Vera Dalton' ×
'Highlight') × 'Merlin'. Large corollas of 30 petals in tones
of pink, shiny leaves.

PRINCESS MICHIKO
by A. Dickson, 1966. Parentage: 'Circus' × 'Spartan'.
Bushy; large, semidouble corollas of 15 petals, cup-shaped,
orange-bronze with yellow eyes, shiny leaves.

PURPLE SPLENDOUR
by Le Grice, 1976. Parentage: 'News' × 'Overture.' Erect;
large corollas of 26 petals, brilliant purple-red, dark leaves.
Slightly fragrant.

PUSSTA
('New Daily Mail') by Tantau, 1972. Parentage: 'Letkis'
× 'Walzertraum'. Vigorous, erect, bushy; large, semidouble
corollas, globular buds.

QUEEN SILVIA
by Meilland, 1980. Medium corollas of 30–35 petals,
vermilion.

Pussta

Redcap

Redgold

Red Cushion

Red Pinocchio

Red Glory

Rendan

Rimosa

Rob Roy

Rosali

REDCAP
by Swim, 1954. Parentage: 'World's Fair' × 'Pinocchio'. Vigorous, erect, bushy; medium, semidouble corollas of 18 petals, ovoid buds, semiglossy, coriaceous leaves.

RED CUSHION
by Armstrong, 1966. Parentage: 'Circus' × 'Ruby Lips'. Vigorous, bushy; small, semidouble corollas, pointed buds, dark, shiny, coriaceous leaves. Slightly fragrant.

RED GLORY
by Swim, 1958. Parentage: 'Gay Lady' × ('Pinocchio' × 'Floradora'). Very vigorous, high, bushy, adapted to hedges; large, semidouble corollas of 11 petals, cup-shaped and flat, in round bunches, ovoid and pointed buds, semiglossy, coriaceous leaves. Slightly fragrant.

REDGOLD
('Dicor', 'Rouge et Or') by A. Dickson, 1971. Parentage: (('Karl Herbst' × 'Masquerade') × 'Faust') × 'Piccadilly'. Vigorous and erect; medium, double corollas in large bunches, gold-edged with intense pink, ovoid buds. Slightly fragrant. All-America Rose Selections award, 1971.

RED PINOCCHIO
by Boerner, 1947. Parentage: seed plant of a yellow 'Pinocchio' × 'Donald Prior'. Vigorous, bushy; large corollas of 28 petals, cup-shaped, velvety carmine-red. Fragrant.

RENDAN
by S. Suzuki, 1987. Parentage: ('Queen Elizabeth' × 'Peace') × ('Sarabande' × 'Amanogawa'). Bushy; semidouble corollas of 15 petals, scarlet-fuchsia on white base and underside.

RIMOSA
by F. Meilland, 1958. Parentage: 'Goldilocks' × 'Perla de Montserrat'. Bushy; semidouble corollas, cream-white.

ROB ROY
('Corob') by Cocker, 1970. Parentage: 'Evelyn Fison' × 'Wendy Cussons'. Large corollas of 30 petals, shiny leaves. Slightly fragrant.

ROSALI
('Tanilasor') by M. Tantau, 1983. Parentage unknown. Bushy; medium corollas of 20 petals, shiny green, medium leaves. No fragrance.

Ruby Lips

Rusticana

RUBY LIPS
by Swim, 1958. Parentage: 'World's Fair' × 'Pinocchio'. Vigorous, bushy, somewhat wide growth; large, semidouble corollas of 18 petals, brilliant cardinal red, ovoid and pointed buds, semiglossy leaves. Slightly fragrant.

RUMBA
by S. Poulsen, 1958. Parentage: 'Masquerade' × ('Poulsen's Bedder' × 'Floradora'). Vigorous, bushy; medium corollas of 35 petals, cup-shaped, poppy-red with yellow centers, ovoid buds, dark, shiny, coriaceous leaves. Light, spicy fragrance.

RUSTICANA
('Poppy Flash', 'Miléna') by Meilland, 1971. Parentage: ('Dany Robin' × 'Fire King') × ('Alain' × Rosa chinensis mutabilis). Vigorous, bushy; large corollas of 20 petals. Light fruity fragrance. Gold Medal Geneva, 1970, and Rome, 1972.

SARABANDE
('Meihand', 'Meirabande') by F. Meilland, 1957. Parentage: 'Cocorico' × 'Moulin Rouge'. Low, bushy; medium, semidouble corollas of 13 petals in large bunches, from cup-shaped to flat, orange-red with yellow stamens, semiglossy leaves. Slightly fragrant. Gold Medal Bagatelle, Geneva, and Rome, 1957, Portland, 1958, All-America Rose Selections award, 1960.

Sarabande

Rumba

SARATOGA

by Boerner, 1963. Parentage: 'White Bouquet' × 'Princess White'. Vigorous, erect, bushy; large corollas of 33 petals, gardenia-shaped, in irregular bunches, shiny, coriaceous leaves. Very fragrant. All-America Rose Selections award, 1964.

SCHERZO

('Meipuma') by Paolino, 1975. Parentage: 'Tamango' × 'Frenzy'. Vigorous, bushy; large corollas of 40 petals, spiraled, brilliant scarlet with white and crimson undersides, dark leaves. Gold Medal Belfast, 1975.

SEVENTEEN

by Boerner, 1959. Parentage: 'Pinocchio' from seed × 'Fashion' from seed. Vigorous, bushy; medium corollas, soft pink-flushed coral.

SHOCKING BLUE

('Korblue') by Kordes, 1974. Parentage: seed plant × 'Silver Star'. Vigorous; double corollas, turbinate, mauve-lilac, dark, shiny, coriaceous leaves. Very fragrant.

SIMPLICITY

('Jacink') by Warriner, 1978. Parentage: 'Iceberg' × unnamed seedling. Compact, columnar growth suitable for hedges; large, semidouble corollas of 18 petals, flat, in numerous bunches, long and pointed buds, medium green leaves. Slightly fragrant.

SIREN

by Kordes, 1953. Parentage: ('Baby Château' × 'Else Poulsen') × 'Independence'. Vigorous, compact; large, semidouble corollas of 18 petals, cup-shaped, ovoid buds, coriaceous leaves. Fragrant. Gold Medal Royal National Rose Society, 1952.

SONORA

by Boerner, 1962. Parentage: 'Orange Mist' × 'Mayday'. Greenhouse variety, vigorous and erect; large corollas, cup-shaped, yellow-brown suffused with pink, coriaceous leaves. Fragrant.

SPANISH SUN

by Boerner, 1966. Parentage: climbing 'Yellow Pinocchio' from seed × 'Golden Garnette'. Vigorous, bushy; large, double corollas, shiny, coriaceous leaves. Very fragrant.

SPRINGFIELDS

('Dicband') by A. Dickson, 1978. Parentage: 'Eurorose' × 'Anabell'. Large corollas of 48 petals, cup-shaped, orange, red, and gold. Slightly fragrant.

Saratoga

Scherzo

Seventeen

Simplicity

Sonora

Shocking Blue

Spanish Sun

Siren

Springfields

Strawberry Crush

Sun Flare

Tabarin

Tamango

STRAWBERRY CRUSH
by A. Dickson, 1974. Parentage: 'Bridal Pink' × 'Franklin Engelmann'. Large, full corollas, red leaves when young. Slightly fragrant.

SUN FLARE
('Jacjem') by Warriner, 1983. Parentage: 'Sunsprite' × seed plant. Low, compact; flat corollas of 30 petals, pointed buds, small, shiny leaves, reddish prickles. Slightly fragrant. Gold Medal Tokyo, 1981, All-America Rose Selections award, 1983.

TABARIN
by Gaujard, 1950. Parentage: 'Opera' × 'Masquerade'. Bushy; semidouble corollas, salmon-pink.

TAMANGO
('Meidanu') by M. L. Meilland, 1967. Parentage: ('Alain' × Rosa chinensis mutabilis) × ('Radar' × 'Caprice').

TASOGARE
by Kobayashi, 1967. Parentage: 'Gletscher' × ('Sterling Silver' × 'Gletscher'). Vigorous with wide growth; large, flat, and semidouble corollas of 18 petals.

Tasogare

Taranga

Tchin-Tchin

Tequila

Träumerei

Valentine

Violet Carson

Viva

Whisky

TARANGA
('Tanagnarat') by M. Tantau, 1981. Bushy; medium, semidouble corollas, semiglossy, medium green leaves. No fragrance.

TCHIN-TCHIN
('Meikinosi') by Paolino, 1978. Parentage: (('Zambra' × 'Suspense') × 'King's Ransom') × ('Kabuki' × 'Dr. A. J. Verhange'). Vigorous; large corollas of 30 petals, cup-shaped, chrome yellow.

TEQUILA
('Meigavesol') by M. L. Meilland, 1982. Parentage: 'Poppy Flash' × ('Rumba' × ('Meikim' × 'Fire King')). Bushy; large, double corollas of 20 petals, light yellow brushed orange, carmine marked on the undersides, dark, opaque leaves.

TRAUMEREI
('Korrei', 'Riekor') by Kordes, 1974. Parentage: 'Colour Wonder' × seed plant. Vigorous, erect, bushy; medium, double corollas, cup-shaped, tapered and pointed buds, coriaceous leaves. Very fragrant.

VALENTINE
by Swim, 1951. Parentage: 'China Doll' × 'World's Fair'. Bushy, compact, wide growth; medium, semidouble corollas of 18 petals in large bunches, dark, olive green leaves. Slightly fragrant.

VIOLET CARSON
('Macio') by S. McGredy IV, 1964. Parentage: 'Mme. Leon Cuny' × 'Spartan'. Compact, bushy; well-formed, medium corollas of 35 petals, peach pink with silver underside, dark, shiny leaves. Fragrant.

VIVA
by Warriner, 1974. Parentage: seed plant × seed plant. Vigorous and erect; medium, double corollas, dark, shiny leaves. Slightly fragrant.

WHISKY
by Delforge, 1964. Parentage: 'Cognac' × 'Arc-en-ciel'. Large corollas, yellow-flushed orange with bronze shades. Slightly fragrant.

WHITE BOUQUET
by Boerner, 1956. Parentage: 'Glacier' × 'Pinocchio' from seed. Bushy; large corollas of 45 petals, gardenia-shaped, in irregular bunches, ovoid buds, dark, shiny leaves. All-America Rose Selections award, 1957.

YACHIYONISHIKI
by S. Suzuki, 1984. Parentage: ('Maxim' × 'Miyojo') × 'Duftwolke'. Double corollas, deep orange.

YELLOW BELINDA
by Tantau, 1972. Parentage: sport of 'Belinda'. Medium, well-formed corollas, deep yellow.

YELLOW CUSHION
by D. L. Armstrong, 1962. Parentage: 'Fandango' × 'Pinocchio'. Vigorous, bushy; large, double corollas in small bunches, shiny, coriaceous leaves. Fragrant.

YELLOW HAMMER
('Yellowhammer', 'Yellow Dazzler') by McGredy, 1956. Parentage: 'Poulsen's Yellow' × seed plant. Greenhouse variety, vigorous, bushy; large corollas of 48 petals, from gold-yellow to pale yellow, dark, shiny leaves. Fragrant. Gold Medal Royal National Rose Society, 1954.

YELLOW PINOCCHIO
by Boerner, 1949. Parentage: 'Goldilocks' × 'Marionette'. Vigorous, bushy; large corollas of 45 petals, cup-shaped, apricot that tends to cream, ovoid buds, dark leaves. Fragrant.

ZAMBRA
('Meialfi') by M. L. Meilland, 1964. Parentage: ('Goldilocks' × 'Fashion') × ('Goldilocks' × 'Fashion'). Vigorous, well-branched; large, flat, semidouble corollas of 13 petals, lively orange with yellow underside, ovoid buds, shiny, clear green, coriaceous leaves. Slight fragrance of Rosa eglanteria.

ZORINA
('Rozorina') by Boerner, 1963. Parentage: 'Pinocchio' from seed × 'Spartan'. Greenhouse variety, vigorous, erect; large corollas of 25 petals, cup-shaped, orange-red, shiny leaves. Fragrant. Gold Medal Rome, 1964.

White Bouquet

Yachiyonishiki

Yellow Belinda

Yellow Pinocchio

Yellow Cushion

Zambra

Yellow Hammer

Zorina

Miniature Roses

Miniature Roses

Today, Miniature Roses find particular favor with an ever-growing public. The reason for this enthusiasm is no doubt to be found in their graceful features, their balanced proportions, the fineness of their minuscule flowers, and their fine and delicate foliage. Their success is also due to their versatility and the fact they take up little space. They are thus suitable to small gardens which are often the only ones we can permit ourselves today. Suitable to being grown in containers, they can be placed in rocky areas and along garden borders, on terraces, and on balconies. Easy to grow and resistant to the cold, they can be grown by anyone, anywhere, and, for a short period of time, they can even be kept in apartments.

Miniature Roses, which resemble Tea shrubs or Floribunda, though they are no taller than fifteen inches, have been popular for some thirty years now. Rosebushes taller than fifteen inches are sometimes called Miniature, but in reality they are impostors. In Europe their history dates to the beginning of the 19th century, while in China, where their family founder was born, their history goes even further back.

In 1821 the English journal *Botanical Register* featured a drawing of a minuscule rose hardly four inches high, said to come from Mauritius Island; the species was called *Rosa pusilla*. Redouté painted the same rose, calling it by another name: *Rosa pumila*. This rose, grown in the Colvill nursery in Chelsea, was rebaptized with its final scientific name, *Rosa chinensis minima*. As was usual with roses new on the scene, this rose became the object of experimentation and hybridization by experts, giving rise to several interesting descendents, among them the still-famous 'Pompon de Paris'.

A step forward was made at the beginning of the 20th century. Major Roulet, a doctor in the Swiss army, one day noticed a very small rosebush on the windowsill of a chalet in a small village of Jura. He held it to be from an unknown species. The botanist Correvon confirmed this and called the rose *Rosa rouletii*, in honor of its discoverer. In truth, however, this rose was no different from *chinensis minima,* and though there was some confusion initially, today authors agree this is it a plant from the same species.

This dwarf rose was not accorded excessive importance in the 19th century. However, in the next century it caught the interest of several rose cultivators including the Dutchman Jan de Vink, the Spaniard Pedro Dot, and the American Robert Pyle. Each of these cultivators began a series of cross-fertilizations with other roses such as the Polyantha, the Tea Hybrids, Chinese roses like the 'Old Blush', and even the rose 'Cécile Brunner', a shrub of modest size with flowers that are perfectly shaped but only as big as a thimble. The hybrids obtained between 1940 and 1950 were a success and are still justly famous today; from Pedro Dot 'Estrellita de Oro', 'Perla de Alcanada', and 'Para Ti', which flowers at a height of two inches; from Pyle 'Sweet Fairy', and 'Peon', later renamed 'Tom Thumb'. A little later another American, Ralph Moore, joined the competition. Having introduced a good number of admirable varieties onto the market ('Lavender Lace' and 'My Valentine'), he obtained mossy Miniature Roses and creeping Miniature Roses by means of unexpected and ingenious crosses.

Various firms have also made their contributions to the production of Miniatures, including Kordes ('Rosmarin' and 'Swergkönig'), Dickson, Cocker, Harkness, McGredy from New Zealand, Suzuki from Japan ('Sazanami', gold-medal-winner at Tokyo in 1980), and de Ruiter ('Bluenette', 1983). Of particular note here is the French firm Meilland, which began with two masterpieces, 'Starina' and 'Colibri'. Today Meilland dominates the international market with its 'Meillandina' found in every color, floriferous and very compact, with single or double flowers. Another fine Miniature from 1982 is Vittorio Barni's 'Tesorino', which is very popular in Italy.

AIR FRANCE MEILLANDINA
('Air France', 'Meifinaro', 'Rosy Meillandina', 'American Independence') by M. L. Meilland, 1982. Parentage: 'Minijet' × ('Darling Flame' × 'Perle de Monserrat'). Bushy; small, double corollas of 40 or more petals, yellow edged in pink, minute, opaque leaves. No fragrance.

APRICOT MEILLANDINA
by Meilland, 1985. Well-formed corollas, orange.

BABY BACCARA
('Meibyba') by Alain Meilland, 1965. Parentage: 'Callisto' × 'Perla de Alcanada'. Small, double corollas, orange-scarlet, dark leaves. Slightly fragrant.

BABY MASQUERADE
('Tanba', 'Tanbakede', 'Baby Carnival', 'Baby Mascarade', 'Baby Maskarade') by M. Tantau, 1956. Parentage: 'Tom Thumb' × 'Masquerade'. Vigorous, compact, 10 inches high; small corollas of 23 petals, yellow tending to red, ovoid buds, coriaceous leaves. Slight fruity fragrance.

BAMBINO
by P. Dot, 1953. Parentage: sport of 'Perla de Alcanada'. Corollas of 25 petals, pink.

Baby Baccará

Baby Masquerade

Apricot Meillandina

Bambino

Air France Meillandina

Belle Meillandina

Bluenette

Cinderella

Colibrì '79

Cream Gold

Easter Morning

Golden Angel

Holy Toledo

Hula Girl

Indian Meillandina

BELLE MEILLANDINA
('Meidanego', 'Belle Sunblaze') by M. L. Meilland, 1980.
Parentage: sport of 'Meillandina' with dark red flowers.

BLUENETTE
('Blue Peter', 'Reiblun', 'Azulabria'), by G. de Ruiter, 1983. Parentage: 'Little Flirt' × seed plant. Bushy; small, semidouble corollas, purple-lilac, tiny, clear green, semiglossy leaves. Slightly fragrant.

CINDERELLA
by de Vink, 1953. Parentage: 'Cecile Brunner' × 'Tom Thumb'. Erect; small corollas of 55 petals, satin white touched with pale pink. Without prickles. Spicy fragrance.

COLIBRI '79
('Meidoanover') by Meilland, 1979. Parentage unknown. Erect and bushy; very double corollas, yellow suffused with pink and orange, medium green, semiglossy leaves.

CREAM GOLD
by R. S. Moore, 1978. Parentage: climbing 'Golden Glow' × unknown. Compact, with wide growth; small corollas of 38 petals, turbinate. Fragrant.

EASTER MORNING
by R. S. Moore, 1960. Parentage: climbing 'Golden Glow' × 'Zee'. Vigorous, dwarf (20 inches); small corollas of 65 petals, ivory white, pointed buds, shiny, coriaceous leaves.

GOLDEN ANGEL
by R. S. Moore, 1975. Parentage: climbing 'Golden Glow' × ('Little Darling' × seed plant). Bushy, compact; small corollas of 65 petals, short, pointed buds, opaque leaves. Fragrant.

HOLY TOLEDO
('Arobri') by Christensen, 1978. Parentage: 'Gingersnap' × 'Magic Carrousel'. Vigorous, bushy; medium corollas of 28 petals, imbricate, brilliant apricot-orange with yellow-orange undersides, ovoid, pointed buds, tiny, dark, shiny leaves.

HULA GIRL
by E. D. Williams, 1975. Parentage: 'Hill Crest' × 'Mabel Dot'. Bushy; small corollas of 45 petals, tapered and pointed buds, tiny, shiny leaves. Fruity fragrance. Certificate of Excellence for Miniatures U.S.A., 1976.

INDIAN MEILLANDINA
('Carol Jean', 'Indian Sunblaze') by R. S. Moore, 1977. Parentage: 'Pinocchio' × 'Little Chief'. Erect, very bushy; small corollas of 22 petals, pointed buds.

Lady Meillandina

Lutin

Lavender Lace

Magic Carrousel

Lavender Meillandina

LADY MEILLANDINA
by Meilland, 1986. Well-formed corollas of 5 petals, pink.

LAVENDER LACE
by R. S. Moore, 1968. Vigorous, bushy, dwarf; small corollas, turbinate, tiny, shiny leaves. Fragrant.

LAVENDER MEILLANDINA
by Meilland, 1985. Corollas lavender on white base.

LUTIN
by Meilland, 1974. Parentage: sport of 'Scarlet Gem'.

MAGIC CARROUSEL
by R. S. Moore, 1972. Parentage: 'Little Darling' × 'Westmont'.

MEILLANDINA
('Meirov') by Paolino, 1975. Parentage: 'Rumba' × ('Dany Robin' × 'Fire King'). Vigorous; small corollas of 20 petals, first cup-shaped then imbricate, currant red.

Meillandina

MEINADENTEL
by Meilland, 1981. Double corollas of 15–20 petals,
near-white pink.

MY VALENTINE
by R. S. Moore, 1975. Parentage: 'Little Chief' × 'Little
Curt'. Vigorous, bushy; small corollas of 65 petals,
turbinate, tiny, shiny leaves with bronze tints.

ORANGE MEILLANDINA
('Orange Sunblaze', 'Meijikatar') by M. L. Meilland,
1982. Parentage: 'Parador' × ('Baby Bettina' × 'Duchess
of Windsor'). Erect, bushy; medium corollas of 35 petals,
cup-shaped, in small bunches, tiny, clear green, opaque
leaves, ochre-brown prickles. Slightly fragrant.

PEEK-A-BOO
('Brass Ring', 'Dicgrow') by P. Dickson, 1981. Parentage:
'Memento' × 'Nozomi'. Erect, with arched branches; flat
corollas of 21 small petals, bronze-orange that pales to pink,
pointed buds, tiny, shiny leaves.

PETITE FOLIE
('Meiherode') by Meilland, 1968. Parentage: ('Dany
Robin' × 'Fire King') × ('Cricri' × 'Perla de
Montserrat'). Vigorous; small, double, globular corollas,
vermilion with carmine underside, coriaceous leaves. Slight
fruity fragrance. Gold Medal Tokyo, 1969.

PINK MEILLANDINA
by M. L. Meilland, 1980. Parentage: sport of 'Orange
Meillandina'. Medium large corollas, salmon-pink.

POMPON DE PARIS
Parentage unknown; variant of the Rosa chinensis
minima, very similar to Rosa rouletii; very small, double
corollas, brilliant pink, very pointed buds, tiny leaves.

RED MEILLANDINA
by Meilland, 1984. Well-formed corollas, ruby red, in
groups of 2–3 flowers.

Meinadentel

My Valentine

Orange Meillandina

Pink Meillandina

Peek-a-Boo

Pompon de Paris

Petite Folie

Red Meillandina

Red Minimo

Rosmarin

Rise 'n' Shine

Sazanami

Scalletta

Scarlet Gem

RED MINIMO
by de Ruiter, 1986.

RISE 'N' SHINE
('Golden Meillandina') by R. S. Moore, 1977.

ROSEMARIN
by R. Kordes, 1965. Parentage: 'Tom Thumb' × 'Dacapo'.

SAZANAMI
by S. Suzuki, 1982.

SCALLETTA
by de Ruiter, 1972.

SCARLET GEM
('Meido', 'Scarlet Pimpernel') by A. Meilland, 1961.

SCARLET MEILLANDINA
('Scarlet Sunblaze', 'Meicubasi') by M. L. Meilland, 1980.

SCHANBIRAN
by Meilland.

STACEY SUE
by R. S. Moore, 1976.

STARINA
('Meigabi') by M. L. Meilland, 1965.

STRIPE MEILLANDINA
by Meilland, 1986.

WHITE GEM
('Meiturusa') by Meilland, 1976.

WHITE MADONNA
by R. S. Moore, 1973.

WHITE MEILLANDINA
('Meiblam', 'Yorkshire Sunblaze') by M. L. Meilland, 1983.

YELLOW DOLL
by R. S. Moore, 1962. Parentage: 'Golden Glow' × 'Zee'.

YELLOW MEILLANDINA
('Meitrisical') by M. L. Meilland, 1980.

YUKIHIME
by Y. Kubota and M. Kubota, 1965.

ZWERGKÖNIG '78
('Dwarfking '78') by Kordes, 1980.

Scarlet Meillandina

Stripe Meillandina

Yellow Doll

Schanbiran

White Gem

Yellow Meillandina

Stacey Sue

White Madonna

Yukihime

Starina

White Meillandina

Zwergkönig '78

Climbing Roses

Climbing Roses

The history of the climbing roses is not as involved as that of the shrub roses. Among the Europeans, the *arvensis* and *sempervirens* are climbers. The Asiatic types are more numerous and include the *gigantea,* the *chinensis,* and the *multiflora,* which have played important roles in the creation of many kinds of roses. Others that have had a lesser role include the *banksiae,* the *laevigata,* the *filipes,* and the *longicuspis.*

Through the ages, art has testified to the cultivation of climbing roses. There are the voluptuous roses that intertwine with cypresses in the gardens of Persian miniatures, and the roses that cover walls in Pompeian frescoes. There are those that serve as a canopy for Madonnas in paintings, and that embrace colonnades and run over shrubs in Romantic prints.

However, the attention of hybridizers has always focused with greater interest on the more common shrub roses, making them more complicated, while leaving the climbing roses in peace. Thus the climbing roses have not given rise to particularly complex species. Climbing roses from the past are represented by several Noisettes and several Pernettianes, and the yellow Tea Hybrids by Pernet Ducher. A notable specimen of ambiguous parentage is the very popular and successful 'Gloire de Dijon', half Bourbon and half Tea.

Three small groups of climbing roses experienced fleeting but well-earned fame in the 19th century, and some of these varieties have come down to us today. The first two groups are the Ayrshire Roses, with unclear origins, though they are certainly descendants of the *Rosa arvensis* and are just as certainly Scottish; and the French Boursault Roses, whose most notable representative is the refined 'Mme. Sancy de Parabère'.

The third group, also French, is formed by several hybrids of the *Rosa sempervirens,* the evergreen rose, which is not very prickly at all and boasts flowers in large clusters. Among this group we find the unbeatable 'Félicité et Perpétue' and 'Adélaide d'Orleans', created by A. A. Jacques, gardener to Louis Philippe before he became king of France.

Modern-day climbing roses are conveniently divided into two distinct groups with very different characteristics: climbers and ramblers.

Climbers are sturdy rose shrubs attaining a height of two to three yards, with a few strong, rigid stems. The flowers are usually individual or in small groups, with medium-sized or large corollas, and are of the perpetual variety.

Ramblers, most of which derive from the *Rosa wichuraiana* and the *multiflora,* are, on the other hand, wilder rosebushes, capable of growing very high—some as tall as twenty yards—and having long, flexible stems that intertwine to form a mass of vegetation. The flowers are usually small and joined in bunches, which can be very large, and have a plentiful flowering, but one that is almost never repeated during the year.

Among the climbers, some forms of the Tea Hybrids, the Perpetual Hybrids, and the Floribunda are important, including both those born as spontaneous mutations as well as those created by hybridizers. In the catalogues and literature they are mentioned as 'Mme. Butterfly', climbing, 'Crimson Glory', climbing, and 'Allgold', climbing. Many of these varieties have shown they are able to carry out their new climbing role very well.

Among the climbing rosebushes many stand alone and cannot be included in any category; it would be impossible to name them all, given their large number, and everyone has his favorite. Some of the more notable include; 'Altissimo', with elegant stamens like large mustaches, a beautiful rosebush especially when allowed to grow horizontally; 'Clair Matin', created by Meilland in 1950, with flowers as exquisite as precious porcelain; 'Golden Showers', one of the best modern-day yellow climbers; 'Meg', with its splendid rippling corollas of indescribable color; and 'Handel', a very reflowering, glossy cream rose. And there are many old varieties that stand up well against more recent creations, particularly 'Spanish Beauty' by Dot, sometimes called 'Mme. Grégoire Staechelin', from 1929, whose fragrance can permeate an entire garden.

Singled out as one of the best climbers of the 1980s was R. Kordes' 'Kordiska', an enchanting, vivid pink flower that slowly fades into peach and apricot. One of the most respected climber producers today is Chris Warner from Newport, Virginia. Among his creations are 'Lady Barbara' and 'Chewizz', which received the Royal National Rose Society's Certificate of Merit.

Of great interest among the ramblers are the *Rosa wichuraiana* hybrids and the *Rosa multiflora* hybrids.

The *Rosa wichuraiana* is an excellent plant for covering the ground. It is a strong climber of Asian origin with glossy leaves and large bunches of single, white flowers. It is called the "memorial rose," as it is often planted near tombs. At the beginning of this century several hybridizers dedicated themselves to this rose, including Manda, Brownell, van Fleet, the firm of Jackson & Perkins in America, and Barbier, in France. Several of their more notable hybrids include: the elegant 'May Queen' (Manda, 1898); 'Dorothy Perkins' (Jackson & Perkins, 1901), charming with its thick rosettes, though very prone to disease; 'American

Pillar' by van Fleet (1902), which gained tremendous popularity; and the much-loved 'Alberic Barbier' and 'Albertine', which have rather large flowers for ramblers. Apart from these successes, there were no further developments. New and interesting forms have been created in more recent years, including; the 'New Dawn' rose, a spontaneous mutation of the old 'Dr. W. van Fleet' with continual bloom and therefore of worldwide interest, 'Coral Dawn' and the graceful 'Bantry Bay'.

The arrival in 1919 from the United States of 'Max Graf', opened up new possibilities. 'Max Graf', a foundling rose whose parents were given as *Rosa rugosa* and a *wichuraiana,* was a supposedly sterile rose from which Kordes miraculously succeeded in obtaining some seeds. When planted, these seeds produced a new rose, justly called *Rosa* × *kordesii,* which in turn produced several hybrids of interest particularly for their Nordic resistance to intense cold and atmospheric abuse.

Standing out among the × *kordesii* hybrids are; 'Leverkusen', which produces a mass of lemon-yellow flowers whose borders are pleasantly dentated; 'Parkdirektor Riggers', one of the most famous crimson-flowered roses; and 'Dortmund', elegant for its white eye that stands out amid the red petals.

Very robust, and useful in the garden for covering large spaces, are the *Rosa multiflora* hybrids. The hybridizer who has contributed the most in developing this rose is William Paul, whose greatest success is perhaps 'Goldfinch'. Created by Turbat in 1916 and possessing a great and aristocratic beauty is a descendent of 'Goldfinch', 'Ghislaine de Féligonde'. The German 'Veilchenblau' stands out for its original color, somewhere between purple, violet, and lavender.

America

Altissimo

American Pillar

ALTISSIMO
('Delmur') by Delbard-Chabert, 1966. Parentage: 'Ténor'
× unknown. Grandiflora Climber; height 1–2 yards; single
corollas of 7 petals, first cup-shaped then flat.

AMERICA
by Warriner, 1976. Parentage: 'Fragrant Cloud' ×
'Tradition'. Grandiflora Climber; medium corollas of 43
petals, imbricate, salmon with lighter underside.

AMERICAN PILLAR
by Van Fleet, 1902. Parentage: (Rosa wichuraiana ×
Rosa setigera) × a Hybrid Perpetual with red flowers.
Vigorous rambler (height 4–6 yards), not perpetual; simple
corollas, carmine-red with white eyes and yellow stamens.

Angela

Blaze

Bischofsstadt Paderborn

Bonbori

Cadenza

ANGELA
by Kordes, 1988. Climber; medium large corollas, pink.

BISCHOFSSTADT PADERBORN
('Fire Pillar') by R. Kordes, 1964. Climber; also classified among the Shrub Roses. Bushy and vigorous (height 1 yard); semidouble, single corollas shaped like small plates, scarlet cinnabar red.

BLAZE
by Kallay, 1932. Parentage: 'Paul's Scarlet Climber' × 'Gruss an Teplitz'. Grandiflora Climber. Very vigorous, perpetual; medium, semidouble corollas, cup-shaped, in large bunches, dark, coriaceous leaves. Slightly fragrant.

BONBORI
by Keisei Rose Nursery, 1973. Parentage: 'Golden Slippers' × ('Joseph's Coat' × 'Circus' climbing). Corollas orange suffused with apricot. Slightly fragrant.

BRILLIANT MEILLANDINA CLIMBING
('Meiranoga'). Corollas orange-vermilion.

CADENZA
by D. L. Armstrong, 1967. Parentage: 'New Dawn' × 'Embers' climbing. Grandiflora Climber. Moderate growth, compact, perpetual; medium, double corollas in bunches, ovoid buds, shiny, dark, coriaceous leaves. Slightly fragrant.

CÉCILE BRÜNNER CLIMBING
by Hosp, 1894. Parentage: sport of 'Cécile Brünner'. Climbing Polyantha. Vigorous (height 6 yards), perpetual; very small corollas, similar to a Hybrid Tea, conchshell pink, tapered and pointed buds. Fragrant.

Brilliant Meillandina Climbing

Cécile Brünner Climbing

Charleston Climbing

Christopher Stone Climbing

CHARLESTON CLIMBING
by Rumsey 1966. Climbing Floribunda.

CHRISTOPHER STONE CLIMBING
by Marsh's Nursery, 1942. Parentage: sport of 'Christopher Stone'. Climbing Hybrid Tea.

CLAIR MATIN
('Meimont') by M. L. Meilland, 1960. Parentage: 'Fashion' × (('Independence' × 'Orange Triumph') × 'Phyllis Bide'). Grandiflora Climber. Vigorous (height 3–3.5 yards), well-branched; medium, semidouble corollas of 15 petals, cup-shaped to flat, pastel pink, pointed buds, dark, coriaceous leaves. Fragrance of Rosa eglanteria. *Gold Medal Bagatelle, 1960.*

COCKTAIL
('Meimick') by F. Meilland, 1957. Parentage: ('Independence' × 'Orange Triumph') × 'Phyllis Bide'. Climber; also classified among the Shrub Roses. Vigorous (height 1 yard), perpetual; medium, single corollas of 5 petals in bunches, geranium red on a primrose yellow base, pointed buds, shiny, coriaceous leaves. Slight, spicy fragrance.

CONFIDENCE CLIMBING
by Hendrickx, 1961. Climbing Hybrid Tea.

CRIMSON CONQUEST
by Chaplin Bros., 1931. Parentage: sport of 'Red-Letter Day'. Climbing Hybrid Tea. Vigorous; small, semidouble corollas, dark, velvety red, dark green leaves.

CRIMSON GLORY CLIMBING
by Jackson & Perkins, 1946. Parentage: sport of 'Crimson Glory'. Climbing Hybrid Tea.

Clair Matin

Crimson Conquest

Cocktail

Confidence Climbing

Crimson Glory Climbing

Danse du Feu

Dr. Huey

Dortmund

DANSE DU FEU

('Spectacular') by Mallerin, 1953. Parentage: 'Paul's Scarlet Climber' × an unspecified Rosa multiflora *from seed. Grandiflora Climber. Vigorous (height 2.5–3 yards), perpetual; medium corollas, from cup-shaped to flat, of 33 petals, in bunches, ovoid buds, shiny bronze leaves. Fragrant.*

DR. HUEY

('Shafter') by Thomas, 1914. Parentage: 'Ethel' × 'Grüss an Teplitz'. Grandiflora Climber. Used as grafting stock; small, semidouble corollas of 15 petals in bunches, intense green leaves. Slightly fragrant.

DOROTHY PERKINS

by Jackson & Perkins, 1901. Parentage: Rosa wichuraiana *× 'Mme. Gabriel Luizet'. Rambler. Very vigorous (height 3–6 yards), not perpetual; small, full corollas, dark leaves.*

DORTMUND

by W. Kordes, 1955. Parentage: seed plant × Rosa kordesii. *Hybrid ×* kordesii. *Vigorous (height 2.5–3 yards), perpetual; large, single corollas in large bunches, red with white eyes, dark, very shiny leaves. Fragrant.*

EASLEA'S GOLDEN RAMBLER

('Golden Rambler') by Easlea, 1932. Grandiflora Climber. Vigorous, not perpetual; large corollas of 35 petals in bunches, yellow-brown marked with crimson, coriaceous leaves.

Dorothy Perkins

Easlea's Golden Rambler

Eden Rose Climbing

Evergold

Exploit

Fure-Daiko

Fireglow Climbing

EDEN ROSE CLIMBING
by Alain Meilland, 1962. Climbing Hybrid Tea.

EVERGOLD
by Kordes, 1956. Medium corollas, deep yellow.

EXPLOIT
('Meilider') by M. L. Meilland, 1983. Parentage: 'Fugue' × 'Sparkling Scarlet'. Grandiflora Climber. Very vigorous, with the tendency to large growth; medium corollas of 20 petals, small, medium green, opaque leaves. No fragrance.

FIREGLOW CLIMBING
by M. Guillot, 1950. Climbing Polyantha. Orange-red corollas.

FRANÇOIS JURANVILLE
by Barbier, 1906. Parentage: Rosa wichuraiana × 'Mme. Laurette Messimy'. Rambler. Very vigorous with large growth; large corollas of unusual form, salmon-pink on a yellow base.

FURE-DAIKO
by Jackson & Perkins, 1974. Parentage: ('Goldilocks' from seed × 'Sarabande') × 'Golden Giant' from seed. Climbing Floribunda.

GARDENIA
by W. A. Manda, 1899. Parentage: Rosa wichuraiana × 'Perle des Jardins'. Rambler. Very vigorous; beautifully formed corollas in small bunches on strong, short stalks, cream-white with yellow centers, pointed yellow buds, small, dark, shiny leaves.

GOLDEN SHOWERS
by Lammerts, 1956. Parentage: 'Charlotte Armstrong' × 'Capt. Thomas'. Grandiflora Climber. Vigorous (height 2–3 yards), perpetual; large corollas of 27 petals, turbinate to flat, single and in bunches, narcissus yellow, tapered and pointed buds, dark, shiny leaves. Fragrant. Gold Medal Portland and All-America Rose Selections, 1957.

François Juranville

Gardenia

Golden Showers

Hagoromo

Hamburger Phoenix

Hanami-Gawa

Haru-Kaze

Handel

High Noon

HAGOROMO
by S. Suzuki, 1970. Parentage: 'Aztec' from seed × 'New Dawn' from seed. Grandiflora Climber.

HAMBURGER PHOENIX
by Kordes, 1954. Parentage: Rosa × kordesii × seed plant. Hybrid × kordesii. Classified also among the Shrub Roses. Vigorous, used as a climber or ground-cover rose, perpetual; large corollas in bunches, deep red, tapered, pointed buds, dark, shiny leaves, large, orange-red fruit. Slightly fragrant.

HANAMI-GAWA
by S. Suzuki, 1986. Parentage: 'Sarabande' from seed × 'Rondo' from seed. Miniature Climbing Rose.

HANDEL
by Sam McGredy IV, 1965. Parentage: 'Columbine' × 'Heidelberg'. Grandiflora Climber. Perpetual; large corollas of 22 petals, cream edged with red, shiny, olive green leaves.

HARU-KAZE
by S. Suzuki, 1985. Parentage: 'Charleston' × 'Dorothy Perkins'. Grandiflora Climber.

HIGH NOON
by Lammerts, 1946. Parentage: 'Soeur Thérèse' × 'Capt. Thomas'. Climbing Hybrid Tea. Erect, vigorous (height 2.5–3 yards); medium corollas of 28 petals, shaped like an open cup, lemon-yellow, shiny, coriaceous leaves. Spicy fragrance.

Honoho-no-Nami

Inspiration

HONOHO-NO-NAMI
by S. Suzuki, 1968. Parentage: 'Spectacular' × 'Aztec'.
Grandiflora Climber. Large corollas of 10 petals.

INSPIRATION
by Jacobus, 1946. Parentage: 'New Dawn' × 'Crimson
Glory'. Grandiflora Climber. Moderate growth; large,
semidouble corollas, large, shiny leaves. Fragrant.

JOSEPH'S COAT
by D. L. Armstrong and Swim, 1964. Parentage:
'Buccaneer' × 'Circus'. Grandiflora Climber. Vigorous,
medium height, perpetual; large, double corollas, red and
yellow, dark, shiny leaves. Slightly fragrant. Gold Medal
Bagatelle, 1964.

Joseph's Coat

Kommodore

Kojo no Tsuki

Lawinia

KOJO NO TSUKI
by K. Teranisi, 1965. Parentage: ('Souvenir de Jacques
Verschuren' × 'Thais') × 'Amarillo'. Grandiflora Climber.

KOMMODORE
('The Commodore') by M. Tantau, 1959. Climber.
Medium large corollas, scarlet. Fragrant.

LAWINIA
('Tanklewi', 'Lavinia') by M. Tantau, 1980. Parentage
unknown. Grandiflora Climber. Height 2.5 yards with wide
growth; large corollas of 20 petals, cup-shaped, medium
green, large, semiglossy leaves. Fragrant.

LITTLE SHOWOFF
by R. S. Moore, 1960. Parentage: 'Golden Glow' × 'Zee'.
Climbing Miniature. Erect (height 1.3 yards); small corollas
of 30 petals, turbinate, brilliant yellow sometimes marked
with red, pointed buds. Fragrant.

Little Showoff

LOOPING
('Meirovonex') by M. L. Meilland, 1977. Parentage:
(('Zambra' × 'Zambra') × ('Malcair' × 'Danse des
Sylphes') × ('Cocktail' × 'Cocktail')) × 'Royal Gold'.
Vigorous; medium corollas of 40 petals, first flat then
cup-shaped, coral-orange, conical buds, dark leaves. Slightly
fragrant. Spring flowering.

LYDIA
by Kordes, 1973. Parentage: seed plant × 'Circus'.
Climber, also classified among the Shrub Roses. Very
vigorous and erect; medium, semidouble corollas, cup-shaped,
intense orange with yellow underside, ovoid buds, dark,
shiny, coriaceous leaves. Fragrant.

MAGIC WANDT
by R. S. Moore, 1957. Parentage: 'Eblouissant' × 'Zee'.
Climbing Miniature. Arched branches, height 1.3 yards;
small corollas of 20 petals, light red, small leaves, dark,
orange fruit.

MARIA CALLAS CLIMBING
('Miss All-American Beauty' climbing, 'Meidaudsar') by
Meilland, 1969. Climbing Hybrid Tea.

MINUETTE CLIMBING
by Kato, 1974. Parentage: sport of 'Minuette'. Climber.

MRS. PIERRE S. DU PONT CLIMBING
by Hillock, 1933. Parentage: sport of 'Mrs. Pierre S. du
Pont'. Climbing Hybrid Tea.

NEW DAWN
('Everblooming Dr. W. Van Fleet') by Somerset Rose
Nursery, 1930. Parentage: sport of 'Dr. W. Van Fleet'.
Characteristics like those of the mother plant, but
reflowering.

NOZOMI
by Onodera, 1968. Parentage: 'Fairy Princess' × 'Sweet
Fairy'. With creeper growth; small, single, flat corollas, pearl
pink, tiny, shiny leaves. Slightly fragrant.

PEACE CLIMBING
('Mme. A. Meilland' climbing) by Brandy, 1950.
Climbing Hybrid Tea.

Looping

Lydia

Magic Wandt

Maria Callas Climbing

New Dawn

Minuette Climbing

Nozomi

Mrs. Pierre S. du Pont Climbing

Peace Climbing

Pink Cameo

Pinkie Climbing

Record

Princess Michiko Climbing

Retro

Royal Scarlet Hybrid

Samourai Climbing

PINK CAMEO
(*'Cameo' climbing*) *by R. S. Moore, 1954. Parentage:* (*'Soeur Thérèse'* × *'Skyrocket'*) × *'Zee'. Climbing Miniature. Height 1–1.6 yards; small corollas of 23 petals, pink with darker centers, tiny, shiny, deep green leaves. Slightly fragrant.*

PINKIE CLIMBING
by Derling, 1952. Parentage: sport of 'Pinkie'. Climbing Polyantha.

PRINCESS MICHIKO CLIMBING
by Keisei Rose Nursery, 1977. Parentage: sport of 'Princess Michiko'. Climber.

RECORD
(*'Decor'*) *by Mallerin, 1951. Parentage:* (*'Love'* × *'Paul's Scarlet Climber'*) × *'Demain'. Climber with large flowers. Vigorous; medium, semidouble corollas, brilliant scarlet, coriaceous leaves.*

RETRO
by Meilland, 1980. Climber. Large, well-formed corollas, deep pink.

ROYAL SCARLET HYBRID
by Chaplin Bros., 1926. Grandiflora Climber. Medium large corollas, slightly rippling petals, dark scarlet.

SAMOURAI CLIMBING
(*'Scarlet Knight' climbing*) *by Jack, 1972. Parentage: sport of 'Samourai'. Climbing Grandiflora.*

Rusticana Climbing

Sarabande Climbing

Seika Climbing

Shin Setsu

RUSTICANA CLIMBING
('Poppy Flash' climbing, 'Meilénasar') by Paolino, 1975.
Parentage: sport of 'Rusticana'. Climbing Floribunda.

SARABANDE CLIMBING
('Meihandsar') by Meilland, 1968. Parentage: sport of
'Sarabande'. Gold Medal Tokyo, 1968.

SEIKA CLIMBING
('Olympic Torch' climbing) by Keisei Rose Nursery, 1985.
Mutation of 'Seika'. Climber.

SHIN SETSU
('Fresh Snow') by S. Suzuki. Parentage: ('Blanche
Mallerin' × 'Neige Parfum') × 'New Dawn' from seed.

Spanish Beauty

Spectra

SPANISH BEAUTY
('Mme. Gregoire Staechelin') by P. Dot, 1927. Parentage:
'Frau Karl Druschki' × 'Chateau de Clos Vougeot'.
Grandiflora Climber. Vigorous (height 4–5 yards), not
perpetual; very large corollas, curled, delicate pink with
undersides marked in crimson, heavy leaves, dark,
pear-shaped fruit. Fragrant. Gold Medal Bagatelle, 1927,
and American Rose Society award, 1929.

SPECTRA
by Meilland, 1983. Climber. Large corollas, deep yellow
edged red.

STARS 'N' STRIPES
by R. S. Moore, 1976. Parentage: 'Little Chief' × ('Little
Darling' × 'Ferdinand Pichard'). Climbing Miniature.
Erect, bushy; corollas of 21 petals, turbinate, with regular
white and red stripes, tapered and pointed buds, light green
leaves. Sweet fragrance.

Stars 'n' Stripes

SUMMER SNOW CLIMBING

by Cocteau, 1936. Parentage: 'Tausendschon' from seed ×
unknown. Climbing Floribunda. Vigorous (height 3.5
yards), irregularly perpetual; medium, semidouble corollas,
cup-shaped, in large bunches, coriaceous leaves. Slightly
fragrant.

TAUSENDSCHÖN

('Thousand Beauties') by J. C. Schmidt, 1906. Parentage:
'Daniel Lacombe' × 'Weisser Herumstreicher'. Rambler
(hybrid of multiflora). Height 3.5 yards; large, double
corollas in large bunches, cup-shaped, dark pink with wide
white centers, soft leaves, no prickles. Slightly fragrant.

ULMER MÜNSTER

('Kortello') by W. Kordes, 1982. Parentage: 'Sympathie' ×
seed plant. Also classified among the Shrub Roses. Large
corollas of 35 petals, dark red, wide, dark, shiny leaves.
Slightly fragrant.

UNCLE WALTER

('Macon') by Sam McGredy IV, 1963. Parentage:
'Detroiter' × 'Heidelberg'. Climber. Vigorous; large corollas
of 30 petals, turbinate, scarlet crimson, coriaceous, bronze
leaves.

VIOLETTE

by Turbat, 1921. Rambler (Hybrid of multiflora).
Vigorous; very double corollas in large bunches, pure violet.

WHITE COCKADE

by Cocker, 1969. Parentage: 'New Dawn' × 'Circus'.
Grandiflora Climber. Vigorous; large, double corollas, shiny
leaves. Fragrant.

ZAMBRA CLIMBING

('Meialfisar') by Meilland, 1969. Parentage: sport of
'Zambra'. Climbing Floribunda.

Summer Snow Climbing

Tausendschön

Ulmer Münster

Violette

Uncle Walter

Zambra Climbing

White Cockade

Shrub Roses

Shrub Roses

It is obvious that the rather generic expression "shrub rose" does not refer to a single type of rose, but is used rather as a convenient category that joins roses of very diverse types and origins. In fact, one thing these roses seem to have in common is that they are not comfortably defined by the characteristics of other groups. However, they do possess a common trait that separates them from rose shrubs like the Hybrid Teas or Floribundas. This trait is a more open and disorderly vegetative growth, with shoots that extend upward or outward for two yards or more.

Their growth and greater height make these so-called shrub roses suitable to garden areas other than rosebeds. They can form small groups or even hedges, be grown as climbers, or placed at the foot of walls or tree trunks. Their effect is perfect in an informal garden.

Shrub roses represent many of the old roses. Among them are: the *Rosa damascena* × *bifera,* also called 'Four Seasons' for its reflowering during the year; another ancient damask, the 'York & Lancaster'; the *centifolia muscosa* 'Chapeau de Napoléon'; the Portland 'Rose du Roi'; the unbeatable Bourbon 'Souvenir de la Malmaison'; 'Blush Noisette', family head of the Noisettes; and 'Maréchal Niel'. Certain older roses and their direct hybrids are also shrub roses, such as 'Canary Birds', which derives from *Rosa xanthina,* or 'Mermaid', which derives from *Rosa bracteata.*

Included in the shrub roses are a great many modern varieties. Some of these modern shrubs exhibit similarities that trace back to an ancestral species. Some, on the other hand, find no place in any other category. This is true of 'Fred Loads', given an award by the Rose Society of London. Nearly six feet tall with truly extravagant flower clusters, 'Fred Loads' was created in 1968 by a dilettante named Holmes. Holmes had already given us

'Sally Holmes', another shrub rose with a very pleasing aspect and well-earned fame. The well-known and beautiful 'Nevada', by Pedro Dot, a descendent from the *Rosa moyesii* and cultivated around the world today, is another example of a rose that could not be categorized comfortably into any of the previously existing groups.

One of the most characteristic species of shrub rose is that of the Hybrid *rugosa.* Having reached Europe at the end of the 18th century, this rose from Japan, China, and Korea, with its charming apple-green foliage crossed by ripples, as if cut out from fabric, attracted the attention of horticulturists only at the end of the last century. One of the first hybrids to appear—many were spontaneous mutations—was 'Hansa', with semi-double and purple corollas. Other hybrids included 'Blanc Double de Coubert', also semi-double and wonderfully fragrant with a scent like violets, and 'Rose à Parfum de l'Hay', double, carmine-red, and very fragrant.

The climb to popular success began with the arrival of 'Scabrosa'. A resistance to cold, the ability to adapt to any kind of soil, even sandy, the surprising effect created by the large tomato-colored fruits that join the flower on the stem, the very cheerfulness of these rose shrubs— these are the qualities that make *rugosa* so loved. In many countries, especially in the north of Europe, they are used to form large, fencelike hedges, which are made impenetrable by the dense growth of sharp prickles. The queen of this group is the very popular 'Frau Dagmar Hastrup', light rose-colored and veined with silver. Also of note are the elegant 'Sarah van Fleet', and the rather unusual 'Pink Grootendorst', whose flowers are like clusters of small pink carnations.

Another very popular group is that of the Hybrid *moschata.* At the turn of the century a great German hybridizer, Peter Lambert, created a small number of robust climbing rosebushes, among them 'Aglaia' and 'Trier', from such *Rosa moschata* descendants as the Noisette Roses and the *Rosa multiflora*. The English Reverend Joseph Pemberton became interested in Lambert's work, and cross-fertilized 'Trier' with Hybrid Teas and Reflowering Hybrids, obtaining the so-called Pemberton Roses, or Hybrid *moschata*. These shrub roses had all the requirements for success: grace and beauty, long supple branches, thick clusters of flowers in charming pastel shades, and generous flowerings. Extremely popular were 'Penelope', a mixture of white, cream, and peach; the pale coral 'Cornelia'; the silver-pink 'Felicia'; and 'Francesca', with large golden-yellow corollas. Succeeding Pemberton was one of his gardeners, J. A. Bentall, who also inherited the garden and the stock of the Reverend's roses. Of particular note is 'Buff Beauty' by Ann Bentall, a splendid apricot-yellow hybrid. Worthy of mention for their quality among the Hybrid *moschata* are Kordes's roses as well: 'Erfurt', 'Berlin', and 'Bonn'.

Also at the turn of the century another group of rosebushes was born, which we list here among the shrub roses. This group is the Penzance Brier, derived from the *Rosa eglanteria* (or *rubiginosa*), famous in England under the name of Brier Rose, and similar to another delightful wild rose, the *canina*. This rose, blooming in summer, possesses a unique quality: it has leaves that, upon rubbing, give an intense apple fragrance. It is to aristocrat Lord Penzance, a lawyer by profession, that credit is due for creating these roses. From crosses between the *eglanteria* and the Perpetual Hybrids, Bourbon Roses, and even the Persian roses (*Rosa foetida*)—which contribute their bold yellow to liven up the color—the Penzance Roses were born. They include 'Lord Penzance', 'Lady Penzance', 'Amy Robsart', 'Meg Merrilies', and 'Julia Mannering'.

Not by Penzance, though nonetheless a daughter of *eleganteria* despite the slight resemblance, is 'Fritz Nobis' (1940), created by the very active Kordes. This rose is of an elegant salmon color, with rippling petals. What a shame it is not reflowering!

Also in the shrub rose category are the Hybrid *spinosissimas,* roses that today are more commonly called by the synonym *Rosa pimpinellifolia*. This is a Scottish rose and therefore very resistant to the cold with a surprisingly black fruit. In Scotland it is known as the Burnet Rose. It has an Asian cousin, from Mongolia and Siberia, called the *Rosa spinosissima altaica*.

In 1793, in the vicinity of Perth, two brothers named Brown found a *spinosissima* rose whose characteristics were of great interest. After several years of patient seedings and selections they obtained promising double forms. Robert Austin, from Glasgow, continued this work in 1814, giving it a new boost. Then, in 1830, to immortalize forever the *Rosa spinosissima* and its offspring, came 'Stanwell Perpetual', a rose somewhat delicate and greatly ruffled (a descendent from an *altaica*). Although not admired by those in search of great effects, it is adored for its more modest beauty. The corollas are like sweetly perfumed, tiny flakes that surround a small green bud peeping out from the center.

By the middle of the 19th century the varieties of *spinosissima* in circulation already numbered more than a hundred, but their fame remained confined to British gardens. In the 20th century, the *spinosissima* hybrids acquired international renown, thanks to Kordes's creation of the group of roses named after spring: 'Fruhlingsgold', a large shrub with long and flexible branches and wide, simple corollas, gilded like the gold of spring; 'Fruhlingsmorgen', radiant as morning; and 'Fruhlingsduft', fragrant as are the others of this type. An American *spinosissima* hybrid not to be ignored is 'Golden Wings', from 1956, which truly does honor to its name.

If all of these shrub roses belong to years long gone by, they proudly stand up to today's competition. David Austin's most recent and successful creations belong to the 1980s. This English rose cultivator has done brilliant work that has made him famous worldwide. Austin started with a well-defined hybridization plan and, armed with patience, began a series of crosses between old roses, such as damask and *gallica,* and modern roses, such as Hybrid Teas and Floribundas. One of the first pleasing results was 'Constance Spry', a rose from 1961 that is still a favorite today. This cultivar presents a wonderful effect with its peony-shaped corollas and embodies all the grace of the roses from the past.

Unfortunately, this cultivar is missing the quality of being perpetual. Possessing this quality instead are Austin's most recent rosebushes, which he has named 'English Roses' and 'New English Roses'. From the 1970s we should mention 'Charles Austin' and 'Chaucer'. In the 1980s, other masterpieces arrived on the scene, such as 'Perdita', of a pale apricot color that blends into pink and white; 'Graham Thomas', burning yellow in color; 'Heritage'; and 'Claire Rose', with its full corollas. All these roses, together with many others, can provide an original and unique collection. Austin's English Roses are often small shrubs, well suited for use in flowerbeds.

Berlin

Bonica

Blanc Double de Coubert

Bonn

Blush Noisette

BERLIN
by Kordes, 1949. Parentage: 'Eva' × 'Peace'. Very vigorous, erect, perpetual; large, single corollas.

BLANC DOUBLE DE COUBERT
by Cochet-Cochet, 1892. Parentage: Rosa rugosa × 'Sombreuil'. Hybrid of rugosa.

BLUSH NOISETTE
by Noisette, 1817. Parentage: obtained from seeds from the rose Champney's 'Pink Cluster'. Whitish pink corollas.

BONICA
('Bonica '82', 'Meidomonac') by M. L. Meilland, 1983. Parentage: (Rosa sempervirens × 'Mlle. Marthe Carron') × 'Piccasso'. Bushy, disease resistant.

BONN
by Kordes, 1950. Parentage: 'Hamburg' × 'Independence'. Hybrid of moschata.

Bourbon Queen

Cardinal de Richelieu

Canary Bird

Chapeau de Napoléon

BOURBON QUEEN
('Queen of Bourbons', 'Reine des Iles Bourbon', 'Souvenir de la Princesse de Lamballe') by Mauget, 1834. Bourbon.

BUFF BEAUTY
by Ann Bentall, 1939. Parentage: 'William Allen Richardson' × unknown.

CANARY BIRD
1907. Parentage: probably a spontaneous hybrid of Rosa hugonis × Rosa xanthina.

CARDINAL DE RICHELIEU
by Laffay, 1840. Parentage unknown; probably created in Holland by Van Sian and known by the name 'Van Sian Rose'. Gallica.

CHAPEAU DE NAPOLEON
('Crested Moss', 'Crested Provence Rose', Rosa centifolia cristata, Rosa centifolia muscosa cristata (Prevost) Hooker) by Vibert, 1827.

Buff Beauty

Commandant Beaurepaire

Cramoisi Supérieur

Comte de Chambord

COMMANDANT BEAUREPAIRE
by Moreau-Robert, 1874. Bourbon. Vigorous, occasionally perpetual; large, double corollas.

COMTE DE CHAMBORD
by Robert & Moreau, 1860. Portland. Vigorous and erect; very full, flat corollas, pink suffused with lilac.

CORNELIA
by Pemberton, 1925. Hybrid of moschata. Very vigorous, perpetual; double corollas formed like rosettes, pale strawberry pink suffused with yellow.

Cornelia

Desprez à Fleurs Jaunes

Echo

CRAMOISI SUPÉRIEUR
('Agrippina') by Coquereau, 1832. Chinese. Vigorous, perpetual; small, double corollas, cup-shaped, in large bunches, crimson-red.

DESPREZ À FLEURS JAUNES
('Jaune Desprez', 'Noisette Desprez') by Desprez, 1830. Parentage: 'Blush Noisette' × 'Park's Yellow Tea-scented China'. Noisette. Vigorous (height 7 yards); double corollas, flat, warm yellow suffused with peach and apricot. Fragrant.

DIRIGENT
('The Conductor') by M. Tantau, 1956. Parentage: 'Fanal' × 'Karl Weinhausen'. Vigorous (height 1 yard), perpetual.

ECHO
('Baby Tausendschon') by P. Lambert, 1914. Parentage: sport of 'Tausendschon'. Hybrid of multiflora.

ERFURT
by Kordes, 1939. Parentage: 'Eva' × 'Réveil Dijonnais'. Hybrid of moschata. Vigorous (height 1.5-2 yards).

Dirigent

Erfurt

Félicité Parmentier

Four Seasons

F.J. Grootendorst

Francesca

Golden Wings

Grootendorst Supreme

Hansa

Henri Martin

FÉLICITÉ PARMENTIER
Cultivated since 1834. Alba. Vigorous, compact; very double corollas that open flat and curve backward, pale pink, gray-green leaves. Very fragrant.

F. J. GROOTENDORST
('Grootendorst', 'Nelkenrose') by de Goey, 1918. Parentage: Rosa rugosa rubra × a Polyantha. Hybrid of rugosa. Vigorous, bushy, perpetual; small corollas in bunches up to 20 flowers, brilliant red with serrated petals similar to those of a carnation, small, coriaceous, dark, rough leaves. Slightly fragrant.

FOUR SEASONS
(Rosa damascena semperflorens *(Duhamel de Courset)* Rowley, Rosa bifera *Persoon,* Rosa damascena bifera, Rosa bifera semperflorens; *'Autumn Damask', 'Quatre Saisons', 'Rose des Quatre Saisons', 'Rose of Castille', 'Castilian', 'Old Castilian'). Damask. Parentage: dates to before 1819. Like 'Summer Damask' but after the summer flowering it reflowers in the fall. Probably the Paestum rose mentioned by classical authors.*

FRANCESCA
by Pemberton, 1922. Parentage: 'Danaë' × 'Sunburst'. Hybrid of moschata. Vigorous (height 1–1.5 yards), perpetual; single corollas in large bunches borne by long runners, apricot, coriaceous leaves. Slightly fragrant.

GOLDEN WINGS
by Shepherd, 1956. Parentage: 'Soeur Thérèse' × (Rosa spinosissima altaica × 'Ormiston Roy'). Vigorous, bushy, very resistant to cold, perpetual; single, large corollas usually of 5 petals, sulphur-yellow with prominent stamens. Slightly fragrant. Gold Medal American Rose Society, 1958.

GROOTENDORST SUPREME
by F. J. Grootendorst, 1936. Parentage: sport of 'F. J. Grootendorst'. Hybrid of rugosa. Corollas of dark crimson red.

HANSA
by Schaum & Van Tol, 1905. Hybrid of rugosa. Vigorous, perpetual, resistant to cold; large, double corollas on short, weak stems, mauve-red, large red fruits. Very fragrant.

HENRI MARTIN
('Red Moss') by Laffay, 1863. Musk. Medium, semidouble corollas, bright scarlet, buds barely mossy.

Hippolyte

Jeanne d'Arc

Kachidoki

HIPPOLYTE
Gallica. Small corollas, lively carmine-red suffused with violet.

JEANNE D'ARC
by Vibert, 1818. Alba. Very dense shrub, height up to 1.5 yards; large, double corollas, between pink and cream tending to ivory-white.

KACHIDOKI
Parentage: sport of 'Dorothy Perkins'. Small corollas of 50-70 petals, scarlet with cream underside. Slightly fragrant.

KING GEORGE IV
('Rivers' George IV', 'George IV') by Rivers, ca. 1817. Parentage: held to be a hybrid between a Damascene Rose and a Chinese Rose. Hybrid of chinensis. Vigorous, branching, not perpetual; double corollas, cup-shaped and open, lively crimson suffused with dark purple, purple branches.

LADY DUNCAN
by Dawson, 1900. Parentage: Rosa wichuraiana × Rosa rugosa. A creeper similar to the 'Max Graf'; not perpetual; medium, single corollas, luminous pink with yellow centers and stamens, shiny leaves.

LA PLUS BELLE DES PONCTUÉES
Gallica. Well-formed corollas, deep pink dotted with pale pink, flat.

LAVENDER LASSIE
by Kordes, 1960. Hybrid of moschata. Very vigorous, tall; medium, double corollas in large bunches, lilac pink. Very fragrant.

LORD PENZANCE
by Penzance, 1894. Parentage: Rosa eglanteria × 'Harrison's Yellow'. Hybrid of eglanteria. Very vigorous; summer blooming; single corollas in bunches, delicate yellow-pink with paler bases, yellow stamens, small, dark leaves. Flowers and leaves are fragrant.

King George IV

La Plus Belle des Ponctuées

Lady Duncan

Lord Penzance

Lavender Lassie

Maréchal Niel

Nevada

Max Graf

Phyllis Bide

Mermaid

Pink Grootendorst

Pink Nevada

Pompon Blanc Parfait

Prince Napoléon

MARÉCHAL NIEL
by Pradel, 1864. Parentage: probably a seed plant of 'Chromatella'. Noisette. Very vigorous, with characteristics of a climber; corollas of 70 petals, large, on weak branches, gold-yellow, tapered and pointed buds, intense green leaves.

MAX GRAF
by Bowditch, 1919. Parentage: probably a hybrid of Rosa rugosa × Rosa wichuraiana. Very bushy, a creeper, not perpetual; medium, single corollas, brilliant pink with white centers, shiny, rough leaves.

MERMAID
by W. Paul, 1918. Parentage: Rosa bracteata × a yellow Tea Rose with double flowers. Hybrid of bracteata. Vigorous, with creeper characteristics (height 1.5–2 yards), irregularly perpetual; large, single corollas of 5 petals, cream-yellow with amber stamens, dark, shiny leaves. Not resistant to cold. Fragrant.

NEVADA
by P. Dot, 1927. Parentage: declared a hybrid between 'La Giralda' and a Rosa moyesii (probably a Rosa moyesii fargesii). Hybrid of moyesii. Vigorous (height 2 yards), bushy, with generous and repeating blooms; single, large corollas on short branches, white with underside sometimes marked with carmine, ovoid buds, pink or apricot in color.

PHYLLIS BIDE
by Bide, 1923. Parentage: 'Perle d'Or' × 'Gloire de Dijon'. Climbing Polyantha. Height 2 yards, irregularly perpetual; corollas are almost double, small, in long, open bunches, pale gold suffused with pink.

PINK GROOTENDORST
by F. J. Grootendorst, 1923. Parentage: sport of 'F. J. Grootendorst'. Hybrid of rugosa. Corollas of clear pink.

PINK NEVADA
('Marguerite Hilling') by Hilling, 1959. Parentage: sport of 'Nevada'. Hybrid of moyesii. Corollas of medium pink.

POMPON BLANC PARFAIT
Introduced in 1876. Alba. Compact; corollas shaped like pompons, pinkish white, almost thornless.

PRINCE NAPOLÉON
Bourbon. Corollas of 30–35 petals, cup-shaped, soft pink.

Sea Foam

Rose à Parfum de l'Hay

Rose du Roi à Fleurs Pourpres

ROSE À PARFUM DE L'HAY
('Parfum de l'Hay',) by Gravereaux, 1901. Parentage:
('Summer Damask' × 'General Jacqueminot') × Rosa
rugosa. Hybrid of rugosa. Vigorous (height 1.5 yards),
perpetual; large, full, globular corollas, cherry-red tending to
blue in warm climates, atypical leaves for a hybrid of rugosa.

ROSE DU ROI À FLEURS POURPRES
Introduced in 1819. Parentage: sport of 'Rose du Roi'.
Portland. Purple corollas.

ST. NICHOLAS
by Hilling, 1950. Parentage: probably a spontaneous hybrid
between Rosa damascena *and a* Rosa gallica, *discovered*
in the garden of R. James. Damask. Vigorous, erect;
semidouble corollas, intense pink.

SEA FOAM
by E. W. Schwartz, 1964. Parentage: (('White Dawn' ×
'Pinocchio') × ('White Dawn' × 'Pinocchio')) × ('White
Dawn' × 'Pinocchio'). Vigorous, perpetual; medium, double
corollas in bunches, from white to cream, tiny, shiny,
coriaceous leaves. Slightly fragrant. Gold Medal Rome,
1963, American Rose Society award, 1968.

St. Nicholas

SHIGYOKU
Gallica. Corollas of 150 small petals, red turning to violet.

SIGNE RELANDER
by S. Poulsen, 1928. Parentage: a hybrid of Rosa rugosa *× 'Orléans Rose'. Hybrid of rugosa. Vigorous (height 2 yards), perpetual; similar to 'Grootendorst Supreme': small, double corollas in bunches, brilliant dark red.*

SKYROCKET
by Kordes, 1934. Parentage: 'Robin Hood' × 'J. C. Thornton'. Hybrid of moschata. Vigorous, bushy (height 2–2.5 yards), perpetual; medium, semidouble corollas in bunches of 50 flowers, tapered and pointed buds, large, shiny, coriaceous leaves. Fragrant.

SOLEIL D'OR
by Pernet-Ducher, 1900. Parentage: 'Antoine Ducher' F2 from seed × Rosa foetida persiana. *Hybrid of foetida; originator of the class of the Pernetianas. Vigorous; large, double corollas, from yellow-orange to golden red suffused with nasturtium red, tapered and pointed buds, deep green leaves. Fragrant.*

SOUVENIR DE LA MALMAISON
('Queen of Beauty and Fragrance') by Beluze, 1843. Parentage: 'Mme. Desprez' × a Tea Rose. Bourbon. Dwarf, bushy, perpetual; very large, double corollas divided in fourths, pink with darker centers. Very fragrant. A climbing form exists (Bennett, 1893).

STANWELL PERPETUAL
by Lee, 1838. Parentage: probably a hybrid of a perpetual Rosa damascena *× a* Rosa spinosissima. *Hybrid of spinosissima. Of modest growth, with a tendency to wide growth; medium corollas, white suffused with pink, tiny leaves; weak branches with many prickles. Slightly fragrant.*

TUSCANY
Before 1820; probably the 'Velvet Rose' of Gerard (1596). Gallica. Vigorous, erect; large, semidouble corollas, from velvety crimson black to dark purple, conspicuous yellow stamens.

VARIEGATA DI BOLOGNA
by Bonfiglioli, 1909. Bourbon. Vigorous (height 2–2.5 yards); large, double, globular corollas in groups of 3–5, white striped with purple-red. Fragrant.

YORK AND LANCASTER
*(*Rosa damascena versicolor *Weston,* Rosa damascena variegata *Thory). In growth before 1629. Damask. Tall; double corollas, open, pink-white to pale pink, with petals of one or the other color or mixed, but not striped, downy, clear gray-green leaves.*

Shigyoku

Signe Relander

Skyrocket

Soleil d'Or

Tuscany

Souv. de la Malmaison

Variegata di Bologna

Stanwell Perpetual

York and Lancaster

Wild Roses

Species, Subspecies, and Hybrid Species

Around 150 species of rose grow wild. They are found over vast areas in the temperate zones, of North America, Europe, Asia and Asia Minor, and Northern Africa. The greatest concentration is found between Western China and the Himalayan Mountains, where 85 percent of the wild species thrive. Today the rose is cultivated and often naturalized all over the world, prospering even in those geographical regions such as Australia and New Zealand where it never before existed in a wild state.

The colors of wild roses range primarily from white to pink, scarlet, and purple; wild yellow roses exist but are less numerous. Wild roses have differing characteristics as far as vegetative growth, preferred environment, and soil quality are concerned. Some are tall and robust shrubs, others dwarfs, while still others are climbers many yards long. Some love calcareous soil, others a more acid one; some grow along the coast in sand while others, like the *palustris,* prefer swamps. Some, like the *spinosissima,* can grow well over a vast area, while others are native to very small locales, such as the *montezuma,* which grows only in New Mexico, and the *glutinosa,* found only in Dalmatia.

The greatest number of naturally occurring yellow-flowered roses are found in the Middle East, where they include the *Rosa haemispherica,* called the Sulphur Rose; the *foetida, foetida persiana,* and *foetida bicolor;* the *kokanica,* which is found as far away as Southern Russia; the *primula,* as far as Central Asia; and the *ecae,* as far as Western China. Originating from this region, and probably also from Europe, North America, and the Himalayas, is the important *Rosa moschata.*

Also from the Himalayas are, among others, the *Rosa brunonii,* of which there exists a Chinese variety, and the *longicuspis.* The Chinese species include the *sericea,* with its characteristic, large, blood-red prickles, the *xanthina* and *hugonis,* which are yellow, the *willmottiae,* the *roxburghii,* the dwarf *farreri persetosa,* the *davidii,* the *macrophylla,* and the *philipes.* Additional Chinese species include the more famous *banksiae, bracteata, wichuraiana, moyesii,* and the very famous—for the part they have played in the history of the development of the rose—*gigantea, multiflora,* and *rugosa.*

From North America we have the *Rosa nutkana, arkansana, palustris, setigera, californica,* the *blanda* with its thornless stems, and the trio of the related *nitida, virginiana,* and *carolina.* Flourishing also in America is the *laevigata,* although it came from China and was naturalized here. Several variants of the wild rose have won a secure place beside their more sophisticated sisters, whether they be subspecies, interspecific spontaneous hybrids, or forms perhaps born from seeds in some garden or nursery. Just a few among these are: the 'Canary Bird', derived from the *Rosa xanthina;* the dazzling and very large *Rosa × anemonoides,* a cross between a *laevigata* and a Tea Rose, created in 1895 by a certain Mr. Schmidt; the *Rosa × highdownensis,* born from the seed of a *moyesii* in 1928, and the other stupendous variant of the *moyesii,* 'Geranium', resplendent in color; the *Rosa × harrisonii,* a probable cross between a *pimpinellifolia* and a *foetida;* the *Rosa × cantabrigiensis,* born from a *hugonis* married with a *sericea;* 'Mrs. Colville', deriving from the *pendulina;* the *Rosa × Paulii,* descendant of *rugosa;* and the very elegant *Rosa × dupontii,* probably a cross between a *gallica,* a *moschata* or an *arvensis.*

We should not expect from these roses still so close to nature the richness, generosity, large flowers, and re-flowering capabilities of the roses man has shaped according to his desire. But they possess other enviable qualities, a grace and purity that join with their simplicity, a touching beauty that springs from their fragility and ephemeral nature.

Rosa acicularis

Rosa acicularis dornröschen

Rosa adianthifolia

Rosa acicularis engelmannii

Rosa agrestis

Rosa alba

Rosa alba maxima

ROSA ACICULARIS
*Lindley (*Rosa fauriei *Lévéille,* Rosa acicularis carelica *(Fries) Matsson,* Rosa carelica *Fries,* Rosa sayi *Schweinitz,* Rosa stricta *Macoun & Gibson,* Rosa korsakoviensis *Leveille,* Rosa acicularis taquetii *(Leveille) Nakai; 'Arctic Rose'). Species. Introduced in 1805. Places of origin: North America, northeast Asia, northern Europe. Spiny shrub, very resistant to cold, height 1 yard, July bloom; single corollas from 1–2.5 inches in diameter, dark pink, pointed fruit. Fragrant.*

ROSA ACICULARIS DORNRÖSCHEN
('Dornröschen') by Kordes, 1960. Parentage: 'Pike's Peak' × 'Ballet'. Hybrid of spinosissima. Erect, well-branched, perpetual; large, double corollas in bunches of up to 10 flowers, from salmon to dark pink with yellow undersides. Fragrant.

ROSA ACICULARIS ENGELMANNII
*(S. Watson) Crépin. (*Rosa × engelmannii *S. Watson,* Rosa melina *Greene,* Rosa engelmannii *Crépin,* Rosa bakerii *Rydberg,* Rosa oreophila *Rydberg. Parentage: probably a spontaneous hybrid of* Rosa nutkana × Rosa acicularis. *Introduced in 1891.*

ROSA ADIANTHIFOLIA
Species. Corollas funnel-shaped, white edged light pink, with narrow, notched petals.

ROSA AGRESTIS
*Savi (*Rosa sepium *Thuillier). Species. In cultivation since 1878. Similar to* Rosa eglanteria. *Places of origin: Europe, northern Africa. Small corollas, pale pink or white.*

ROSA ALBA
*Linnaeus (*Rosa usitatissima *Gaterau,* Rosa procera *Salisbury; 'White Rose of York', 'Bonnie Prince Charlie's Rose', 'Jacobite Rose'). Parentage: probably a hybrid of* Rosa corymbifera × Rosa gallica. *In cultivation before 1597. Large shrub, height up to 2.5 yards, summer blooms, not perpetual; corollas more or less double, white, usually united in groups, gray-green leaves, ovoid scarlet fruits. Fragrant.*

ROSA ALBA MAXIMA
('Alba Maxima', 'Maxima'). Before 1867. Alba. Height up to 2.5 yards; corollas similar to 'Maiden's Blush' but with cream centers. Originator of the mutation Rosa alba semiplena.

Rosa alba semi-plena

Rosa x andersonii

Rosa arkansana

Rosa alba "Petite Cuisse de Nymphe"

ROSA ALBA PETITE CUISSE DE NYMPHE
('Small Maiden's Blush') by Kew, 1797. Hybrid of alba. Parentage: probably a hybrid of Rosa alba × Rosa centifolia. Distinct from 'Great Maiden's Blush': vigorous.

ROSA ALBA SEMI-PLENA
('Alba Semi-plena'). Alba. Parentage: very ancient form, sport of Rosa alba maxima. Before 1867.

ROSA × ANDERSONII
('Andersonii'). Parentage: accidental hybrid of Rosa canina × probably Rosa arvensis. Introduced in 1935. Wide growth; medium corollas 2–2.5 inches in diameter, single, pink.

ROSA ARKANSANA
Porter (Rosa rydbergi Greene, Rosa suffulta Greene, Rosa heliophila Greene, Rosa pranticola Greene, Rosa arkansoides Schneider, Rosa angustiarum Cockerell). Species. Place of origin: North America. In cultivation since 1880.

ROSA BANKSIAE ALBA
Hort. (Rosa banksiae banksiae, Rosa banksiae alba-plena Rehder; 'White Banksia'). Species. Introduced by William Kerr in 1807. Vigorous climber, semirustic.

Rosa banksiae alba

ROSA BANKSIAE LUTEA

*Lindley (*Rosa banksiae luteaplena *Rehder). Species. Introduced in 1824. Vigorous climber, height 10–12 yards; small, double corollas, butter-yellow. Slightly fragrant.*

ROSA BANKSIAE NORMALIS

Regel. Species. Place of origin: western China, at an altitude of 1500 meters. Introduced in 1796. Vigorous climber.

ROSA BOISSIERII

Crépin. Similar to the Rosa canina.

ROSA BRACTEATA

*Wendland (*Rosa lucida *Lawrance,* Rosa macartnea *Dumont de Courset; 'Maccartney Rose', 'Chickasaw Rose'). Species, sometimes confused with* Rosa laevigata. *Places of origin: China, naturalized in the southeast of North America. Introduced in 1793 by Lord Maccartney. Large shrub, climber or rambler, very prickly, early summer bloom, reflowering in autumn.*

ROSA CALIFORNICA

*Chamisso & Schlechtendahl (*Rosa gratissima *Greene). Species, very variable. Places of origin: western areas of North America. Cultivated since 1878. Vigorous shrub (height 2 yards), blooms middle June to early July.*

ROSA CANINA

*Linnaeus (*Rosa leucantha *Loiseleur,* Rosa pseudoscabrata *Blocki,* Rosa sphaerica *Grenier,* Rosa surcolosa *Woods; 'Brier Bush', 'Dog Rose'). Species, very variable. Places of origin: Europe, sporadically naturalized in North America. In cultivation since 1737. Vigorous shrub (height 3–3.5 yards).*

ROSA CANINA × ROSA GALLICA

Natural hybrid from an early date that has produced many varieties, including some with double, semidouble corollas and varying pink color. Bushy, height up to 2 yards.

ROSA CENTIFOLIA

*Linnaeus (*Rosa gallica centifolia *Regel; 'Provence Rose', 'Cabbage Rose', 'Painter's Rose'). Centifolia, considered a hybrid with a complex origin. In cultivation since 1596. Shrub of medium vigor (height 1.5 yards), summer bloom, not perpetual; large corollas, very double, with overlapping petals, on weak stems and with pronounced sepals, deep pink, large leaves with large serration. Very fragrant.*

ROSA CENTIFOLIA MUSCOSA

*(Aiton) Seringe. (*Rosa muscosa *Aiton; 'Moss Rose'). Musk. Parentage: sport of* Rosa centifolia. *In cultivation before 1750. Shrub of medium vigor (height 1 yard), blooms in the second half of June, not perpetual.*

Rosa banksiae lutea

Rosa banksiae normalis

Rosa californica

Rosa boissierii

Rosa canina

Rosa bracteata

Rosa canina x Rosa gallica

Rosa centifolia muscosa

Rosa centifolia

Rosa centifolia parvifolia

Rosa chinensis

Rosa chinensis alba

Rosa chinensis "Miss Lowe"

Rosa chinensis "Hermosa"

ROSA CENTIFOLIA PARVIFOLIA

*(Ehrhart) Rehder (*Rosa parvifolia *Ehrhart,* Rosa burgundensis *Weston,* Rosa burgundica *Ehrhart,* Rosa remensis *De Candolle,* Rosa ehrahrtiana *Trattinick,* Rosa pomponia *Thory ex Redouté,* Rosa gallica remensis *Wallroth;* 'Burgundian Rose', 'Pompon de Bourgogne'). *Centifolia in cultivation since 1664. Dwarf shrub (height up to 1 yard), thick, with small, contorted branches, blooms in the first half of June, not perpetual; very small corollas in the form of rosettes, dark pink suffused with purple with paler centers, gray-green leaves, few prickles. Fragrant.*

ROSA CHINENSIS

*Jacquin (*Rosa sinica *Linnaeus,* Rosa indica *Loureiro,* Rosa chinensis indica *(Lindley) Koehne,* Rosa nankinensis *Loureiro,* Rosa indica vulgaris *Lindley;* 'China Rose', 'Bengal Rose'). *Species. Place of origin: China. In cultivation since 1759. Vigorous climber, perpetual; crimson or pink corollas, rarely white, on long branches, often in bunches, almost evergreen leaves, ovoid fruit.*

ROSA CHINENSIS ALBA

Major variety of the Rosa chinensis. *Vigorous, semiclimber; corollas soft pink at center fading to white. The presence of pigment intensifies the color during blooming and distinguishes it from other chinensis.*

ROSA CHINENSIS HERMOSA

('Hermosa', 'Armosa', 'Melanie Lemaire', 'Mme. Newmann'*) by Marcheseau, 1840. Hybrid of China Rose. Vigorous, perpetual; corollas of 35 petals, small, pink tending to blue, fragrant, green-gray leaves.*

ROSA CHINENSIS MINIMA

*(Sims) Voss (*Rosa semperflorens minima *Sims,* Rosa laurentiae *Trattinick,* Rosa lawranceana *Sweet,* Rosa indica pumila *Thory). Sometimes called* 'Fairy Rose'. *In cultivation since 1815. Group of Chinese dwarfs, of variable heights, with white corollas, pink or red, single and double, up to 1.5 inches in diameter. Varieties:* Rosa rouletii, *introduced by Correvon in 1922, and* 'Pompon de Paris', *introduced in 1839.*

ROSA CHINENSIS MISS LOWE

('Miss Lowe'*). Parentage: probable sport of* 'Slater's Crimson China'. *Hybrid China. Dwarf shrub, perpetual; single corollas, brilliant red. Confused with* 'Sanguinea', *which has double corollas.*

Rosa chinensis minima

Rosa chinensis "Old Blush"

Rosa chinensis viridiflora

Rosa chinensis semperflorens

Rosa chinensis "Single Pink"

ROSA CHINENSIS OLD BLUSH
('Old Blush', 'Common Monthly', 'Common Blush China', 'Old Pink Monthly', 'Parson's Pink China'). China. Introduced in Sweden in 1752 and in England before 1759. Vigorous, erect, perpetual; semidouble corollas, medium, in two shadings of pink. Barely fragrant.

ROSA CHINENSIS SEMPERFLORENS
(Curtis) Koehne (Rosa semperflorens Curtis, Rosa diversifolia Ventenat, Rosa indica semperflorens (Curtis) Seringe, Rosa bengalensis Persoon; 'Crimson China Rose', 'Chinese Monthly Rose', 'Slater's Crimson China', 'Old Crimson China'). Chinese. Shown in an illustration from 1733 held in the British Museum; introduced by Slater in 1792. Dwarf shrub, extremely perpetual, with semidouble corollas, cherry-red, on thin branches. Intensely fragrant.

ROSA CHINENSIS SINGLE PINK
Chinese hybrid. Corollas 2.5–3 inches in diameter, first pink then, before the loss of petals, a deeper color. Fragrant.

ROSA CHINENSIS VIRIDIFLORA
(Lavalle) Schneider; 'Green Rose'). Chinese. In cultivation before 1845. Of medium vigor, erect (height 1 yard), perpetual; very double corollas, with narrow, long petals, green, often suffused with bronze, in small bunches.

Rosa chinensis "Single Pink"

Rosa cinnamomea

Rosa cocanica

Rosa cinnamomea plena

Rosa damascena

ROSA CINNAMOMEA

Linnaeus (Rosa collincola Ehrhart; 'Cinnamon Rose').
Species. Places of origin: Europe, northern and western
Asia. In cultivation before 1600. Height 2 yards, blooms
May–June; corollas of 2 inches in diameter, purple.

ROSA CINNAMOMEA PLENA

Weston (Rosa foecundissima Muenchhausen, Rosa
majalis Herrmann; 'Double Cinnamon', 'Steven's Rose').
Species. In cultivation since 1596. Double form of the Rosa
cinnamomea Linneaus. Young branches are purple.

ROSA COCANICA

Regel (Rosa xanthina Lindley var. cocanica Boulenger).
Species. Single corollas, deep, bright yellow. Abundant
flowering.

ROSA DAMASCENA

Miller (Rosa calendarum Borkhausen, Rosa polyanthos
Roessig, Rosa belgica Miller, Rosa gallica damascena
Voss, Rosa bifera Persoon; 'Summer Damask', 'Damask
Rose'). Damask, of garden origin. Introduced in Europe
from Asia Minor during the 16th century. Vigorous shrub
(height 1 yard).

ROSA × DUPONTII

Deseglise (Rosa moschata nivea Lindley, Rosa freudiana
Graebner; 'Dupontii'). Parentage: probably a cross between a
Rosa gallica and a hybrid of Rosa moschata. Perhaps
identical to the 'Spanish Musk Rose' of 1629. Raised by
M. Dupont in France and in cultivation since 1817.
Vigorous shrub (height 2 yards), with wide growth, blooms
early in summer.

Rosa ecae

Rosa foetida

ROSA ECAE
Aitchison (Rosa xanthina Auth., Rosa xanthina ecae (Aitchison) Boulanger). Species. Place of origin: Afghanistan. Introduced in 1880. Shrub of medium vigor (height up to 2 yards), blooms May–June; small corollas (1 inch in diameter), single, deep yellow, on short peduncles, delicate, gray-green leaves, ovoid fruit.

ROSA FOETIDA
Herrmann (Rosa lutea Miller, Rosa eglanteria Miller, Rosa chlorophylla Ehrhart; 'Austrian Brier Rose', 'Austrian Yellow'). Species. Place of origin: Asia. Probably introduced before 1542. Erect, with disorderly growth, blooms in early June, not perpetual; single corollas (2–2.5 inches in diameter), brilliant yellow, globular fruit. Fragrance is unpleasantly sweet.

Rosa x dupontii

Rosa foetida bicolor

Rosa foetida x "Trier"

Rosa foetida persiana

Rosa x fortuniana

Rosa fujisanensis

Rosa x francofurtana

Rosa gallica

Rosa gallica officinalis

ROSA FOETIDA BICOLOR
(Jacquin) Willmott (Rosa lutea punicea (Miller) R. Keller, Rosa punicea Miller, Rosa bicolor Jacquin, Rosa lutea bicolor Sims, Rosa eglanteria punicea Thory, Rosa aurantiaca Voss; 'Austrian Copper'). Species. Parentage: sport of Rosa foetida.

ROSA FOETIDA PERSIANA
(Lemaire) Rehder (Rosa lutea persiana Lemaire, Rosa lutea plena hort., Rosa hemisphaerica plena Rehder; 'Persian Yellow'). Species. Parentage: probably a sport of Rosa foetida. Place of origin: probably Iran.

ROSA FOETIDA × TRIER
('Star of Persia') by Pemberton, 1919. Hybrid of foetida. Vigorous (height 2–3 yards); medium, semidouble corollas, brilliant yellow with golden stamens.

ROSA × FORTUNIANA
Lindley (Rosa fortuneana Lemaire; 'Fortuniana', 'Fortuneana', 'Double Cherokee'). Parentage: probable hybrid of Rosa banksiae × Rosa laevigata. Introduced in 1850. Climber; large, double corollas, white.

ROSA × FRANCOFURTANA
Muenchausen (Rosa turbinia Aiton, Rosa germanica Gordon et al., Rosa campanulata Ehrhart. Rosa francofurtensis Roessig, Rosa inermis Thory). Parentage: probable hybrid of Rosa cinnamomea × Rosa gallica. Introduced before 1629. Summer bloom; single or double corollas (2–2.5 inches in diameter).

ROSA FUJISANENSIS
Makino (Rosa luciae fujisanensis Makino). Single corollas (1–3 inches in diameter), heart-shaped, white.

ROSA GALLICA
Linnaeus (Rosa austriaca Crantz, Rosa olympica Donn, Rosa rubra Lamarck, Rosa sylvatica Gaterau, Rosa grandiflora Salisbury; 'French Rose'). Species. Places of origin: central and southern Europe and western Asia. In cultivation before 1500. Shrub of medium height, summer bloom; corollas deep pink to crimson.

ROSA GALLICA OFFICINALIS
Thory (Rosa provincialis Miller, Rosa gallica plena Regel, Rosa gallica maxima hort., Rosa officinalis (Thory) Kirshleger, Rosa centifolia provincialis; 'Apothecary's Rose', '(The) Apothecary's Rose of Provins', 'Double French Rose', 'Red Rose of Lancaster', 'Officinalis'). Gallica. Probably in cultivation before 1600. Shrub of medium vigor, well-branched, height up to 1 yard, blooms in late June.

Rosa gigantea

ROSA GALLICA VERSICOLOR
*Linnaeus (*Rosa gallica rosa mundi *Weston,* Rosa gallica variegata *Thory,* Rosa mundi*; 'Rosa Mundi'). Parentage: sport of* Rosa gallica officinalis. *Probably in cultivation before 1581. Shrub of medium height (up to 1 yard); semidouble corollas.*

ROSA GIGANTEA
*Collet (*Rosa × odorata gigantea *(Collet ex Crepin) Rehder & Wilson,* Rosa macrocarpa *Watt,* Rosa xanthocarpa *Watt ex Willmott). Species. Places of origin: southwestern China, Burma. Introduced in 1889. Vigorous climber (height up to 8 yards), not resistant to cold, blooms second half of June; large, single corollas (up to 5 inches in diameter).*

Rosa x hardii

Rosa x harisonii

Rosa x harisonii vorbergii

ROSA × HARDII
Cels (× 'Hulthemosa hardii' *(Cels) Rowley). Parentage:* Hulthemia persica × Rosa clinophylla. *Introduced by Hardy before 1836.*

ROSA × HARISONII
*Rivers (*Rosa lutea hoggii *Don,* Rosa foetida harisonii *Rehder; 'Harrison's Yellow'). Hybrid of foetida. Parentage: probably a hybrid of 'Persian Yellow' ×* Rosa spinosissima. *Introduced around 1830.*

ROSA × HARISONII VORBERGII
*Rehder (*Rosa vorbergii *Graebner & Spaeth; 'Vorbergii'). Parentage:* Rosa foetida × Rosa spinosissima. *Semidouble corollas, pale yellow.*

Rosa gallica versicolor

Rosa x highdownensis

ROSA × HIGHDOWNENSIS

Hillier ('Highdownensis'). Parentage: obtained from seeds of a Rosa moyesii. *Introduced by Sir Frederich Stern in 1928. Vigorous, bushy, height and width about 3 yards; single corollas in bunches, brilliant red, dark leaves, bronze, orange-scarlet fruit, colored prickles. Barely fragrant.*

ROSA HIRTULA

*(Regel) Nakai (*Rosa roxburghii hirtula *(Regel) Rehder & Wilson,* Rosa microphylla hirtula *Regel). Species, similar to* Rosa roxburghii. *Place of origin: Japan. Introduced before 1880. Corollas lily pink, small and delicate leaves, downy on the undersides.*

ROSA HUGONIS

*Hemsley (*Rosa xanthina *Crepin; 'Father Hugo Rose', 'Golden Rose of China'). Species. Place of origin: central China. Introduced in 1899. Vigorous shrub (height and width 2 yards), with arched branches, blooms end of May to early June; single corollas (1–1.5 inches in diameter), shaped like plates, canary yellow on thin peduncles, delicate leaves composed of 11 leaflets, globular, scarlet fruit.*

ROSA × IWARA

*Siebold ex Regel (*Rosa × jesoensis *(Franchet & Savatier) Makino; 'Iwara'). Parentage:* Rosa multiflora × Rosa rugosa. *In cultivation before 1830. Small, single corollas, white.*

ROSA JÁSMINOIDES

*Koidzumi (*Rosa luciae *Franchet et Rochebrune var.* hakonensis *Franchet et Savatier,* Rosa hakonensis *(Franchet et Savatier) Koidzumi).*

ROSA KOREANA

Komarov. Species. Place of origin: Korea. Introduced in 1917. Solitary and numerous corollas (1 inch in diameter) along branches, white suffused with pink, ovoid, orange-red fruit.

Rosa hirtula

Rosa hugonis

Rosa koreana

Rosa x iwara

Rosa jasminoides

Rosa laevigata

Rosa laevigata rosea

Rosa x l'heritierana

Rosa luciae

Rosa x maikai

Rosa marretii

ROSA LAEVIGATA

Michaux (Rosa sinica *Aiton,* Rosa cherokeensis *Donn,* Rosa ternata *Poiret,* Rosa nivea *De Candolle,* Rosa camellia *hort.,* Rosa tryphylla *Roxburgh,* Rosa hystrix *Lindley;* 'Cherokee Rose'). *Species. Places of origin: China, naturalized in the southeast of North America.*

ROSA LAEVIGATA ROSEA

Species. Variant of Rosa laevigata *Michaux. Large corollas (4 inches in diameter), pale pink.*

ROSA × L'HERITIERANA

Thory (Rosa reclinata *Thory,* Rosa boursaultii *hort.;* 'Boursault Rose'). *Group of hybrids, called Rose Boursault, probably derived from crosses between* Rosa chinensis *and* Rosa pendulina, *before 1820.*

ROSA LUCIAE

('Azuma-ibara', 'Oofuj bara', 'Yamatelihano-ibara'). *Species. Places of origin: Japan, on dry, rocky, and hilly terrain; there are also other forms in Taiwan, continental China, and the Korean peninsula.*

ROSA× MAIKAI

Hybrid with double corollas (2.5 inches in diameter), fuchsia to violet.

ROSA MARRETII

Leveille (Rosa rubrostipullata *Keller). Species. Place of origin: Sahalin. In cultivation before 1908.*

ROSA × MICRUGOSA

Henkel (Rosa vilmorinii *Bean,* Rosa wilsonii *A. T. Johnson;* 'Micrugosa'). *Parentage: hybrid of* Rosa roxburghii × Rosa rugosa, *before 1905.*

Rosa x micrugosa

Rosa moschata

Rosa moyesii "Eos"

Rosa moyesii "N. 2"

ROSA MOSCHATA

*Hermann (*Rosa ruscinonensis *Grenier & Deseglise;* 'Musk Rose'). Species. Places of origin: southern Europe, northern Africa (information concerning its wild distribution is uncertain). Introduced in 1540. Vigorous shrub or climber, with spreading growth, with long climbers up to 3 yards, blooms summer-fall; single corollas, white, in corymbs of 7 flowers, shiny and glabrous leaves, composed of 7 segments, ovoid, small fruit. Intense musk fragrance. The* Rosa moschata nepalensis *Lindley or* Rosa brunonii *is a variant, originally from the Himalayan region, introduced in Europe in 1822.*

ROSA MOYESII EOS

('Eos'*) by Ruys, 1950. Parentage:* Rosa moyesii × Rosa rubiginosa magnifica. *Vigorous shrub with climbers, up to 2 yards, not perpetual; medium, semidouble corollas, cup shaped, brilliant red with white centers, in groups, coriaceous, shiny leaves. Slightly fragrant.*

ROSA MOYESII N. 2

*(*Rosa moyesii *Hemsley & Wilson,* Rosa macrophylla rubrostaminea *Vilmore,* Rosa fargesii *Osborn). Species. Place of origin: western China. Introduced in 1894 and reintroduced in 1903. Vigorous and erect shrub (height 3 yards), with arched climbers and strong prickles, blooms in June, not perpetual; corollas (1.5–3 inches in diameter) of deep blood red to dark pink to light pink, solitary or in pairs, flask-shaped, orange-red fruit. No fragrance.*

ROSA MULTIFLORA

*Thunberg (*Rosa thungergii *Trattinnick,* Rosa linkii *Denhardt,* Rosa polyantha *Siebold & Zuccarini,* Rosa thyrsiflora *Leroy ex Deseglise,* Rosa intermedia *Carriere,* Rosa wichurae *K. Kock,* Rosa microcarpa *hort.,* Rosa multiflora thunbergiana *Thory,* Rosa dawsoniana *Ellwanger & Barry ex Rehder,* Rosa franchetii paniculigera *(Makino) Koidzumi;* 'Multiflora Japonica'). Species. Places of origin: eastern Asia, naturalized in North America. Introduced around 1810. Vigorous shrub or climber with long arched climbers (height up to 3 yards), blooms in summer; corollas in large pyramidical corymbs, usually white, leaves composed of 9 segments, small, oval, red fruit. Fragrant.*

Rosa multiflora

Rosa multibracteata

ROSA MULTIBRACTEATA
Hemsley & Wilson (Rosa reducta Baker). Species. Place of origin: western China. Introduced in 1910. Shrub of medium vigor, with delicate and arched branches.

ROSA MULTIFLORA VAR. ADENOCHAETA
(Koidzumi) Ohwi (Rosa polyantha adenochaeta).

ROSA MULTIFLORA PLATYPHYLLA
(Thory) Rehder & Wilson (Rosa cathayensis platyphylla (Thory) Bailey, Rosa thoryi Trattinnick, Rosa platyphylla (Thory) Takasima; 'Seven Sisters', 'Seven Sisters Rose'). Hybrid of multiflora. Introduced in 1817. Corollas from pale pink to crimson, far larger than in Rosa multiflora.

ROSA MULTIFLORA WATSONIANA
(Crepin) Matsumura (Rosa watsoniana Crepin; 'Bamboo Rose'). Species. Introduced in a Japanese garden in 1870. Curious variant of Rosa multiflora, with linear leaves similar to those of a Japanese maple with miniature corollas.

ROSA NIPPONENSIS
Crépin (Rosa acicularis nipponensis (Crepin) Koehne, Rosa acicularis glabra Franchet et Savatier. Species. Place of origin: Japan. Introduced in 1894. Single corollas (1.5 inches in diameter), light scarlet or scarlet-violet. Fragrant.

ROSA NIPPONENSIS × RUGOSA
Hybrid between two species from Japan. Single corollas (2.5–3 inches in diameter) in groups of 3–5 flowers, pink turning to purple. Slightly fragrant.

ROSA NITIDA
Wildlenow (Rosa rubrispina Bosc ex Poiret, Rosa redutea rubescens Thory, Rosa blanda Pursh). Species, very variable. Places of origin: North America from Newfoundland to Massachusetts. In cultivation since 1807. Dwarf shrub (height about 1 foot) with numerous, thorny branches, blooms first half of July; single corollas (2 inches in diameter) on weak peduncles, deep pink, in small corymbs, shiny leaves composed of 9 segments, with splendid autumnal coloring of brilliant red, round fruit.

ROSA NITIDA × ROSA RUGOSA
Hybrid very similar to Rosa rugosa, 2.5–3 inches in diameter, fuchsia.

Rosa multiflora var. adenochaeta

Rosa multiflora platyphylla

Rosa nipponensis x rugosa

Rosa multiflora watsoniana

Rosa nitida

Rosa nipponensis

Rosa nitida x Rosa rugosa

Rosa nutkana

Rosa onoei

Rosa paniculigera

Rosa x paulii

Rosa x paulii rosea

Rosa pendulina

Rosa pendulina x Rosa marretii

Rosa x penzanceana

ROSA NUTKANA
Presl (Rosa manca Greene, Rosa spaldingii Crépin, Rosa muriculata Greene. Species. Places of origin: North America, from Alaska to Utah. Introduced about 1876. Vigorous shrub with branches up to 2 yards.

ROSA ONOEI
Makino (Rosa luciae onoei Kitamura, Rosa hakonensis onoei Koidzumi). Species. Single corollas (¾–1 inch in diameter), white, 2–3 per branch.

ROSA PANICULIGERA
Makino et Momiyama (Rosa luciae paniculigera (Koidzumi) Momiyama). Species: Single corollas (¾–1 inch in diameter), white.

ROSA × PAULII
Rehder. (Rosa rugosa repens alba Paul; 'Paulii'). Parentage: Rosa arvensis × Rosa rugosa. Raised by G. Paul before 1903 in England. Shrub with prostrate characteristics, with height of 36 inches and width of 1.5 yards, very prickly, abundant blooms in June.

ROSA × PAULII ROSEA
Hort. (Rosa rugosa repens rosea; 'Paulii Rosea'). Parentage: probable sport of Rosa × paulii. A little before 1912. Less vigorous than 'Paulii', not perpetual; single corollas, medium pink with white eyes and yellow stamens, with petals of characteristic form. Slightly fragrant.

ROSA PENDULINA
Linnaeus (Rosa alpina Linnaeus, Rosa glandulosa Bellardi, Rosa fraxinifolia Borkhausen; 'Alpine Rose'). Species. Places of origin: central and southern Europe. In cultivation since 1683. Dwarf shrub (maximum height 1 yard), almost without prickles, blooms from the end of June to August; single corollas (2 inches in diameter), usually solitary.

ROSA PENDULINA × ROSA MARRETII
Upright shrub, height 2 yards, steles without prickles, reddish brown; corollas (2–2.5 inches in diameter) of around 20 petals, deep pink, dark green, rippling leaves.

ROSA × PENZANCEANA
Rehder ('Lady Penzance') by Penzance, 1904. Parentage: Rosa eglanteria × Rosa foetida bicolor. Hybrid of eglanteria. Very vigorous and thorny shrub, height up to 1.5 yards, blooms in June, not perpetual; single corollas, salmon-pink with copper shadings, yellow center and stamens, dark leaves composed of small segments. Intense apple fragrance.

Rosa persica

Rosa phoenicia

Rosa pomifera

ROSA PERSICA

Michaux (Hulthemia persica (Michaux) Bornmueller, Rosa berberifolia Pallas, Rosa simplicifolia Salisbury, Hulthemia berberifolia (Pallas) Dumortier, Lowea berberifolia (Pallas) Lindley. Hulthemia is a monotypical genus included by many authors in the genus Rosa, from which it is distinguished by its single leaves, without stipules, and by the small flowers marked with a dark eye.

ROSA PHEONICIA

Boissier. Species. Place of origin: Asia Minor. Introduced around 1885. Similar to Rosa moschata; not resistant to cold; corollas in large corymbs.

ROSA POMIFERA

Herrmann (Rosa villosa Linnaeus, Rosa hispida Poiret; 'Apple Rose'). Species. Places of origin: Europe, western Asia. Introduced in 1771. Vigorous shrub (height and width over 1 yard), with long arched branches, summer blooms; pink corollas, in groups of 1–3.

ROSA PRIMULA

Boulenger (Rosa ecae Kanitz, Rosa sweginzowii Meter, Rosa xanthina Auth., Rosa xanthina normalis Rehder & Wilson). Species. Places of origin: from Turkestan to northern China. Introduced in 1910.

ROSA PRIMULA × REVERSA

Semiupright shrub, 1 yard in height, with prickleless branches; single corollas (1–1.5 inches in diameter), deep pink.

ROSA × RICHARDII

Rehder (Rosa sancta Richard, Rosa centifolia sancta Zabel; 'St. John's Rose'). Species. Parentage: spontaneous hybrid of Rosa gallica × Rosa phoenicia. Place of origin: Abyssinia. In cultivation since 1902.

ROSA ROULETII

Correvon ('Rouletii'). Parentage: variety of Rosa chinensis minima in cultivation before 1818, discovered by Major Roulet in 1918 in Switzerland.

ROSA ROXBURGHII

Trattinnick (Rosa microphylla Roxburgh ex Lindley, Rosa roxburghii plena Rehder; 'Chestnut Rose', 'Chinquapin Rose', 'Burr Rose'). Species. Place of origin: eastern Asia. In cultivation before 1814. Vigorous shrub, height and width 2–3 yards.

ROSA ROXBURGHII NORMALIS

Rehder & Wilson ('Single Chestnut Rose'). Species. Introduced in 1908. Single corollas.

Rosa primula

Rosa rouletii

Rosa primula x reversa

Rosa roxburghii

Rosa x richardii

Rosa roxburghii normalis

Rosa rubiginosa

Rosa rubrifolia

Rosa rubiginosa magnifica

Rosa x ruga

Rosa rugosa

Rosa rugosa alba

Rosa rugosa albo-plena

Rosa rugosa kamtchatica

ROSA RUBIGINOSA
Linnaeus (Rosa eglanteria Linnaeus, Rosa suavifolia Lightfoot, Rosa walpoleana Greene, 'Sweet Brier Rose', 'Eglantine'). Species.

ROSA RUBIGINOSA MAGNIFICA
(Rosa eglanteria duplex Weston, 'Magnifica', Hesse 1916). Parentage: spontaneous birth from a seed of 'Lucy Ashton'.

ROSA RUBRIFOLIA
Villars (Rosa glauca Pourret, Rosa ferruginea Deseglise, Rosa lurida Andrews, Rosa ilseana Crépin).

ROSA × RUGA
Lindley ('Ruga'). Parentage: rose of the Ayrshire group, held to be a hybrid of Rosa arvensis × a Chinese or Tea.

ROSA RUGOSA
Thunberg (Rosa ferox Lawrance, Rosa regeliana Linden & Andre; 'Rugosa Rose', 'Ramanas Rose', 'Japanese Rose', 'Kiska Rose', 'Hedgehog Rose'). Species.

ROSA RUGOSA ALBA
Rehder (Rosa rugosa albiflora Koidzumi). Species.

ROSA RUGOSA ALBO-PLENA
Rehder. Species. White, double corollas.

ROSA RUGOSA KAMTCHATICA
(Ventenat) Regel (Rosa kamtchatica Ventenat). Species.

ROSA RUGOSA PINK
Species. Probably a wild mutation of Rosa rugosa.

Rosa rugosa "Pink"

Rosa rugosa plena

Rosa rugosa x Rosa marretii

Rosa rugosa x Rosa wichuraiana

ROSA RUGOSA PLENA
Regel (Rosa rugosa rubro-plena Rehder, Rosa pubescens Baker, 'Empress of the North'). Species. Shrub very resistant to cold; double corollas, purple.

ROSA RUGOSA × ROSA MARRETTI
Single corollas (2.5–3 inches in diameter), paler fuchsia pink than Rosa rugosa.

ROSA RUGOSA × ROSA WICHURAIANA
Natural hybrid. Place of origin: discovered in the Fukushima prefecture, Honshu, Japan. Shrub with long branches, like the Rosa wichuraiana, with many large and small prickles; corollas (¾–1 inch in diameter), pink or light scarlet with rippling petals that are heart shaped or similar to carnations, many clustered flowers.

ROSA RUGOSA SALMON PINK
Parentage: sport of Rosa rugosa. Corollas pale salmon, in other characteristics identical to the standard type.

Species, Subspecies, and Hybrid Species

Rosa spinosissima

Rosa sericea

Rosa sambucina

Rosa rugosa scabrosa

ROSA RUGOSA SCABROSA

Horr, ('Scabrosa'). Parentage unknown. Introduced by Harkness in 1950. Vigorous, very bushy (height 1 yard); large corollas of 5 petals in groups of 5 or more, mauve-pink with clear, sulphur-yellow stamens, light leaves, shiny, soft, large, brilliant red fruit. Carnation fragrance. Perpetual, with blooms from spring to autumn.

ROSA SAMBUCINA

Single corollas (1.5 inches in diameter), white, heart-shaped petals.

ROSA SERICEA

Lindley (Rosa wallichii Trattinnick, Rosa tetrapetala Royle). Species. Places of origin: regions of the Himalayas, western China. Introduced in 1822. Shrub of 4 yards in height; blooms in early spring; corollas (1–2 inches in diameter), white with 4 petals, rarely 5, globular or turbinate fruit. Sweet fragrance.

ROSA SERICEA HEATHER MUIR

('Heather Muir'). Species. Variant of Rosa sericea. Introduced by the Sunningdale Nursery in 1957. Corollas (3 inches in diameter) of pure white, with long blooms, single, finely subdivided leaves, orange fruit.

ROSA SETIGERA

Michaux (Rosa trifoliata Rafinesque, Rosa finestrata Donn, 'Prairie Rose'). Species. Place of origin: North America. Introduced in 1810. Shrub-climber with curved runners, height of 3 yards; corollas (2 inches in diameter), pink-red that pales to white, in small corymbs, globular fruit. Summer bloom. No fragrance.

ROSA SPINOSISSIMA

Linnaeus (Rosa pulchella Salisbury, Rosa illinoensis Baker, 'Scotch Rose', 'Burnet Rose'). Species. Places of origin: Europe, western Asia, naturalized occasionally in North America. In cultivation before 1600. Height 1 yard; corollas (1–1.5 inches in diameter) cream, but rose, yellow or purple in garden forms, numerous along the branches, globular, black fruit. Blooms in spring.

ROSA SPINOSISSIMA ALTAICA

(Willdenow) Bean (Rosa altaica Willdenow, Rosa spinosissima baltica hort, Rosa sibirica Trattinnick, Rosa grandiflora Lindley, 'Altaica'). Species. Place of origin: western Asia. Introduced around 1820. More vigorous and with more open growth than Rosa spinosissima, single, large, white corollas, serrated leaves, gray-green, black-maroon fruit in autumn.

Rosa spinosissima altaica

Rosa setigera

Rosa sericea "Heather Muir"

ROSA SPINOSISSIMA DOUBLE PINK

Double or semidouble corollas (1–1.5 inches in diameter) of around 20 petals, pale pink.

ROSA SPINOSISSIMA DOUBLE WHITE

Double corollas, white. Very fragrant.

ROSA SPINOSISSIMA LUTEA

Bean. Species. Considered a hybrid by some authors. Place of origin: Asia. Similar to altaica but less vigorous and with smaller flowers. Corollas are brilliant yellow, single.

ROSA SPINOSISSIMA LUTEA MAXIMA

Corollas (1–1.5 inches in diameter) deep yellow, single.

ROSA STELLATA MIRIFICA

(Greene) Cockerell (Rosa mirifica Greene; 'Sacramento Rose'). Species. Place of origin: North America (New Mexico and Texas). Introduced in 1916. Low and dense shrub; red-purple corollas, ivory bristles at many knots of the branches.

ROSA UCHIYAMANA

Machino (Rosa multiflora cathayensis Rehder & Wilson, Rosa cathayensis (Rehder & Wilson) Bailey). Species. Place of origin: China. Introduced in 1907. Wild form with simple pink corollas (1.5 inches in diameter), with petals separated from one another, cream or white-flushed-pink in spots, grouped in clusters of 20 flowers.

ROSA VILLOSA

Linnaeus (Rosa pomifera Herrmann, Rosa hispida Poiret; 'Apple Rose'). Species. Places of origin: Europe, western Asia. Introduced in 1771. Height 2 yards; pink corollas (1.5–2 inches in diameter) in groups of 1 to 3, ovoid fruit, bristly. Summer bloom.

ROSA VIRGINIANA

Miller (Rosa lucida Erhart, Rosa lucida alba hort., Rosa humilis lucida (Erhart) Best, Rosa pennsylvanica Andrews. Species. Place of origin: North America, from Newfoundland to Pennsylvania. Introduced before 1807. Height 2 yards; brilliant pink corollas (2 inches in diameter), solitary or in small groups, shiny leaves, red fruit that last the entire winter. Summer bloom.

Rosa spinosissima "Double Pink"

Rosa spinosissima "Double White"

Rosa spinosissima lutea

Rosa villosa

Rosa virginiana

Rosa stellata mirifica

Rosa uchiyamana

Rosa spinosissima lutea maxima

Species, Subspecies, and Hybrid Species

Rosa wichuraiana

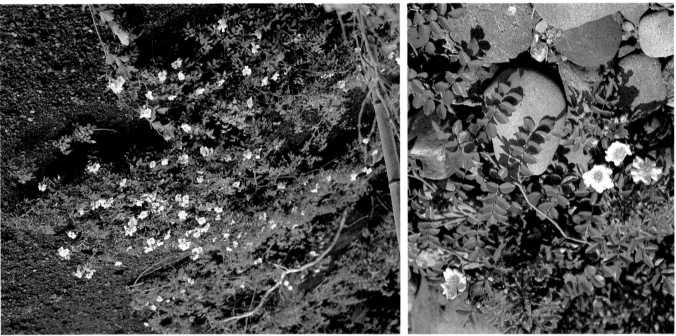

ROSA WICHURAIANA

Crépin (Rosa luciae Franchet & Rochebrune, Rosa luciae wichuraiana (Crépin) Koidzumi, Rosa raquetii Léveillé, Rosa mokanensis Léveillé, Rosa luciae raquetiana Boulenger, Rosa bracteata hort.; 'Memorial Rose'). Species. Place of origin: eastern Asia. Introduced in 1891. Vigorous, semievergreen, with long low runners; white corollas (1.5–2 inches in diameter), in small pyramidal corymbs, ovoid fruit. Fragrant. Blooms in late summer.

ROSA WILLMOTTIAE

Hemsley. Species. Place of origin: western China. Introduced in 1904. Height 1–3 yards; pink-purple corollas (1–2 inches in diameter), solitary, on short peduncles and on short lateral branches, finely subdivided leaves, globular fruit, brilliant red-orange. Spring bloom.

ROSA XANTHINA

Lindley (Rosa xanthinoides Nakai). Species. Places of origin: northern China, Korea. Introduced in 1906. Height of 3 yards; yellow corollas (1¾ inches in diameter), solitary, on short peduncles.

ROSA YAKUSHIMAENSIS

('Rosa Yakualpina'). Corollas (½–¾ inches in diameter), white, single, petals separate from one another.

ROSA YAKUSHIMAENSIS HIMURO

Double corollas of 20 petals, white. Abundant bloom.

Rosa yakushimaensis "Himuro."

Rosa yakushimaensis

Rosa xantina

Rosa willmottiae

Rose Organizations and Contests

Many countries around the world have chapters of The Association of the Friends of the Rose or of The Society of the Rose. Particularly active are the English and American organizations, respectively the Royal National Rose Society (Chiswell Green, St. Albans AL2 3NR Hertfordshire, in existence since 1860), and The American Rose Society (P.O. Box 30,000, Shreveport, Louisiana). These two organizations publish yearly indexes of the roses created, registered, and introduced onto the market. The American edition is entitled Modern Roses, and both are precious reference texts for all the information regarding the parentage and characteristics of an enormous number of varieties.

Credit for the first official rose exhibition goes to the English. The first National Rose Show was held in London in 1858, and was repeated each year from 1860 on, at the Crystal Palace. International competitions began a little later; the first took place in the Bagatelle Gardens, near Paris, in 1907. Other cities soon followed Paris's example, with exhibits that spurred hybridizers and encouraged rose producers and rose lovers. For years now prestigious competitions have been held in Baden Baden, Belfast, Copenhagen, Dublin, Geneva, The Hague, Lyons, Orleans, Madrid, Portland (Oregon), Tokyo, New Zealand, Belgium, Le Roeulx castle, Genoa, Monza, and in Rome since 1933.

Competitions draw professional hybridizers and rose firms, and even private individuals and amateurs present their most recent creations. Varieties are registered, and medals and titles are awarded. There are awards for numerous superior characteristics, including fragrance, and the honor of such awards can contribute to the success and popularity of those roses that receive them. Gold, silver, and bronze medals are also awarded by the Rose Society of Great Britain, in addition to Awards of Merit and the special titles of Rose of the Year and Golden Rose. Prestigious American awards are conferred under various names by The American Rose Society, perhaps most notably the All-America Rose Selections. At its triennial meetings, the World Federation of Rose Societies also proclaims "The World's Favourite Rose."

The World's Great
Rose Creators

Modern roses are a creation of man, not nature. Each of them, like a book, painting, fashionable suit, or piece of music, bears the name of an author on its identity card. The creation of a new rose requires time and a variety of qualities on the part of the creator: sensitivity, instinct, imagination, manual ability, constancy, and diligence, in addition to the ability to wait patiently and accept the absence of results. It is therefore only right that the names of these authors, who should be granted the same honor due any artist, be given the consideration they have earned so that they can become better known.

The professions of the hybridizer and cultivator of new rose varieties often run in families—children and grandchildren frequently follow in the steps of their fathers and grandfathers. The largest rose enterprises in the world tend to be old firms, some founded as long ago as the 19th century, the management of which has passed through three or four generations.

In addition to the large nurseries of the 19th century that laid the foundations for what today is a flourishing industry, many people the world over—from Europe to Africa, the United States to Australia, Canada to India, Portugal to Poland—have contributed their cleverness, their love, and their unflagging efforts to the creation of that enchanting creature called the rose.

The names of Antoine and Francis Meilland stand out among the creators of roses in the 20th century. Today the firm they created distributes new cultivars all through the U.S. and Europe. Meilland's brilliant career began with a number of Tea Hybrids that were enormously successful: 'Peace', 'Grand'mère Jenny', 'Bettina', 'Baccara', 'Eden Rose', 'Maria Callas', and 'Pharaoh'; and with the Floribunda 'Zambra' and 'Rusticana'. This firm's popularity has never waned, and during the 1980s there were further successes that included 'Catherine Deneuve', 'Louis de Funès', and 'Princesse of Monaco'. Today, the name of Meilland is linked particularly to the production of Miniature Roses, the famous 'Meillandina'.

Francis Meilland deserves recognition for having fought to have roses recognized as works of art. For many years now, varieties on the market have been protected by copyright, and their reproduction without proper consent is prohibited. Alain Meilland is credited as creator of 'Papa Meilland', 'Starina', and 'Darling Flame'; the activities of Marie Louise Meilland and Paolino belong to more recent years.

Other notable French rose cultivators include Georges Delbard, whose 'Orange Delbard' marked a new epoch, and Jean Gaujard, to whom we are indebted for 'Rose Gaujard', winner of a gold medal from the RNRS in 1958. Charles Mallerin, who was Francis Meilland's teacher, dedicated himself to roses only after having left his railroad job. An amateur with firm instincts, he began to attract attention in 1931 with 'Editor McFarland'. In 1947 he achieved notable success with his very pure (white, without any color spots) 'Virgo', repeating this success in 1954 with 'Beauté'.

A fundamental contribution to the creation of new roses was given by two families from Northern Ireland: the Dicksons and McCredys. The Dicksons, Alexander and Patrick, worked mainly with the Tea Hybrids, seeking to obtain ever more beautiful flower shapes, though they also dedicated themselves to Teas with single corollas, the famous 'Irish Single'. Dickson roses have won several awards for such triumphs as 'Grandpa Dickson', 'Irish Fireflame', 'Red Devil', and 'Bonsoir'. The McCredys are hybridizers of exceptional expertise who have devoted themselves to roses for four generations. The successes of Sam McGredy in the 1930s came from roses that were unforgettable for their color shades, among them 'McGredy Yellow', 'McGredy Ivory', and 'Sam McGredy', with its purple leaves. These were followed by a wave of celebrities: 'Piccadilly', 'Milord', and 'Mischief'. In 1972 Sam McGredy immigrated to New Zealand, attracted by a milder climate that can be an essential factor in speeding up production at nurseries.

When it comes to flowers and gardens, Great Britain is still at the head of the list, for its technical capabilities, passion, and dedication. The contribution made in the 19th century by Henry Bennett to the creation and study of the Tea Rose Hybrids is a benchmark. Today Great Britain offers perhaps the greatest number of hybridizers, cultivators, and purveyors who specialize in Old and Modern Roses.

Standing out among the most illustrious names is that of Walter Gregory, who began to produce roses in the 1950s; his 'Wendy Cussons' won five important awards. Jack Harkness, vice-president of the Royal National Rose Society and author of many books, continued the rose hybridization and cultivation work begun in 1879 by his grandfather. Harkness has created more than 150 roses; the firm operates at a pace of 2,000 hybrids a year. Among his more famous roses are 'Alexandra', 'Elizabeth Harkness', the Floribundas 'Anne Harkness', 'Escapade', and 'Lake Como', the graceful 'Margaret Merril', and the Polyantha 'Yesterday'.

Also highly successful have been the roses of the Scotsman Alexander Cocker, among them 'Silver Jubilee', for which the hybridizer used the *Rosa kordesii*, thus bringing new blood into the family of the Tea Hybrids. Edward B. Le Grice of Norfolk is another English-man to be included among eminent rose cultivators. He dealt in particular with yellow roses, and his masterpiece is 'Allgold'. Other Floribundas of his that have stood the test of time include such charming roses as 'Dainty Maid' and 'Dusky Maiden' from 1940, and 'Lilac Charm' from 1952, of a fascinating mauve-pink hue. 'My Choice' won numerous awards for Le Grice.

David Austin is a contemporary rose expert of great ingenuity. His famous Romantic 'English Roses' are distributed throughout the world, the result of able crosses between ancient and modern roses. Of equal stature is Peter Beales, author of texts on classic roses and on those of the 20th century. In 1981 Beales created a sumptuous Tea Hybrid, 'Anna Pavlova', which won an award at Genoa. It had an exquisite rose color and was very suitable to temperate climates.

The Germans are important producers of roses. Among the giants are Kordes di Sparrieshop and Tantau di Uetersen. Mathias Tantau began by working on the Polyanthas and Polyantha Hybrids. His son (who has the same name) created a series of very popular Tea Hybrids: 'Prima Ballerina', 'Fragrant Cloud', with a stirring fruit fragrance, and 'Duke of Windsor'; 'Polar Star', from 1980, was named Rose of the Year in Great Britain. Tantau also attempted to produce a blue rose, though blue it is not, with 'Blue Moon'.

The rose owes perhaps even more to A. Wilhelm Kordes. Continuing the work of Pernet-Ducher, Kordes concerned himself particularly with yellow roses, Tea as well as Floribunda, obtaining new, splendid colors in shades of orange and geranium. His roses possess great vigor, strength, and resistance to cold and disease. Kordes's firm worked on other types of roses also. Beginning with the *Rosa spinosissima*, Wilhelm created the group of roses that bear the name of spring, the 'Frühlings', an irreplaceable contribution to the informal garden. Also of his creation are the × *kordesii* roses, such as 'Leverkusen' and 'Parkdirektor Riggers', which are resistant to everything. Other ever-popular successes are 'Crimson Glory', from 1935, 'Karl Herbst', 'Kordes Perfecta', and 'Peer Gynt', from the 1950s. There were further successes by Reimer Kordes, Wilhelm's son, especially with Floribunda roses 'Schneewittchen' and 'Lilli Marlene'. Today a new generation controls this firm.

Holland, a leading country in the world of floriculture, has her share of names in the rose field. The Ruiter father-and-son duo have distinguished themselves in the production of Polyanthas and, later, of Floribundas. Today the firm mainly supplies roses to the Nordic market. Another Dutch firm that is very active today is Interplant.

It was at the Poulsen nurseries, in Denmark, that the Floribundas were born. These are corymb roses—the queens of the flowerbed, the embodiment of a notable event in the history of the rose. Many of the first Floribundas bear the family surname ('Else Poulsen', 'Kirsten Poulsen', 'Yellow Poulsen'), and other names such as that of the charming 'Chinatown', from 1963. Poulsen's main objective was to create roses that were resistant to low temperatures.

From Belgium it is Louis Lens, who succeeded his father in 1945, who is most worthy of mention. 'Pascali' and 'Dame de Coeur' are two of his successes, and his work today particularly involves hybrids of *Rosa moschata*.

As far as the United States is concerned, an important

name on the American market from the 1930s onward is the firm of Jackson & Perkins. Excellent hybridizers have worked for Jackson & Perkins, among them Boerner, whose Floribundas delighted the entire world: 'Goldilocks', 'Lavender Pinocchio', 'Fashion', 'Masquerade', and 'Diamond Jubilee', a Tea Hybrid much acclaimed in 1947. Famous hybridizers have contributed to the success of the Armstrong Nurseries, in California. Lammerts, for example, created such internationally famous roses as 'Chrysler Imperial', 'American Heritage', and 'Queen Elizabeth'. Other names connected with Armstrong are Jack E. Christensen, A. E. Ellis, T. Hansen, and, above all, Herbert Swim, who in the 1950s and 1960s created enormously successful roses, including 'Sutter's Gold', 'Buccaneer', and 'Pink Parfair'.

Ralph Moore is the acclaimed inventor of the mossy and creeping Miniature Roses. Mention should also go to William Warriner, Dee Bennett, Annette Dobbs, and Chris Warner. We must add, however, that a tremendous number of American roses have not easily made their way across the ocean to be known and cultivated by Europeans.

The Japanese also excel in the production of roses. We are in debt to Onodera for a jewel of a rose, the Lilliputian 'Nozomi', from 1968, which is much loved and grown throughout Europe. Emerging during the 1980s are Kaichiro Ota, who became known in 1985 with 'Lucky Choice', and S. Suzuki, to whom we are indebted for the exotically named roses 'Eiko', 'Kan-Pai', (gold medal-winner at Rome in 1980), 'Hi-Ohgi', and 'Hoku-To'.

The preeminent names in Spain are Pedro Dot and his son Simon. The 'Nevada', a rose of worldwide popularity, was born in the Dot nurseries in Penedes. The Dot nurseries developed many of the most beautiful and award-winning Miniature Roses.

Of note in Australia is the work of Alister Clark, who has to his credit some one hundred roses, most of which are unfortunately not found in Europe. This hybridizer has particularly dedicated himself to roses adapted to temperate climates.

In Italy, there are several individuals who stand out who have made, and continue to make, strong contributions to the creation of new roses. Domenico Aicardi became well known in 1936 with 'Saturnia', a gold-medal-winner at Rome and Portland. He repeated his success in 1937 with a brilliant scarlet rose with a cherry-colored underside, 'Gloria di Roma'. The Mansuinos of Sanremo (the leading Italian province for floriculture) are associated with 'Purezza', a rambler that won the gold medal at Rome in 1960. Then there is Bartolomeo Embriaco, also from Sanremo, who created the Miniature 'Isella' (1973), the Floribunda 'Cosetta' (1984), and the Tea Hybrid 'Patrice' (1985). Also working out of Sanremo is Gabriella Lantero, and working out of Ventimiglia is Giuseppe Grossi, who was the gardener at Villa Hanbury and at La Mortola. Distinguishing himself in 1982 with 'Gingia' was Niso Fumagalli, who for many years was the director of the Italian Association of the Rose, and who is an impassioned rose cultivator as well as the founder of the rose garden at the Villa Reale in Monza.

Rose Gardens of the World

There is a great number of public gardens where one can admire and come to know roses of all kinds: old and modern, botanical species and their hybrids, and a seemingly unending line of recent varieties. These gardens include botanic gardens, rose association gardens, the gardens and private parks of castles and estates, and municipal and public gardens.

Very often, the larger developers and purveyors dedicate a portion of their firm's land for exposition purposes and keep rose collections that can be visited. Many of the world's gardens dedicated to roses are true rose gardens and rosariums, exclusively cultivated with these plants. Some display hundreds of specimens (there are more than 12,000 rosebushes in the park of the Grange in Geneva); others, instead, are quite small. Large estates generally dedicate only part of their parks to rose terraces and rosebeds.

The list below, though fairly exhaustive, obviously cannot be considered complete.

AUSTRALIA
Adelaide, The Botanic Garden
Hobart, Tasmanian Rose Society Garden
Melbourne, Royal Botanic Garden
South Yarra (Victoria), Royal Botanic Garden
St. Kilda (Victoria), Alister Clark Rose Garden, St. Kilda Public Gardens
Willunga, W. A. Ross Roses, Andrew's Terrace

AUSTRIA
Baden, Österreichisches Rosarium
Linz, Rosen Garten
Vienna, Donau Park

BELGIUM
Brussels, Château de Beloeil
Ghent, Citadel Park
Hainault, Rosarium Château Roeulx
Limburg, Ghent Rozentuin Koningin Astridpark
Steenweg, International Rozentium

CANADA
Burlington (Ontario), Centennial Rose Garden

Hamilton, The Ontario Royal Botanic Gardens
Montreal, The Floralies Rose Garden; Connaught Park Rose Garden
Niagara, The Canadian Royal Horticultural Society Rose Garden
Ottawa, Dominion Arboretum and Botanic Gardens
Pickering (Ontario), Pickering Nursery
Victoria (British Columbia), Butcharts Gardens
Watertown (Ontario), Hortico, Inc., Nursery

DENMARK
Copenhagen, Valby Park, Tivoli Garten

FEDERAL REPUBLIC OF GERMANY
Baden-Baden, Kurgarten Lichtentaler Allee
Coburg, Rosengarten
Dortmund, Deutsches Rosarium Westfalen Park
Frankfurt am Main, Palmengarten
Hannover, HerrenHausen
Karlsruhe, Rosengarten
Lake Constance, Insel Mainau Rosengarten
Saarbrucken, Rosengarten
Torgau, Kassel Rosengarten

Uetersen, Rosarium
Weimar, Sangerhausen Rosarium
Zweibrucken, Rosengarten

FRANCE
Chalons-sur-Saone, Parc Saint-Nicholas
Choisy, Château de la Malmaison
Lyon, Roseraie du Parc de la Tete d'Or
Nice, Retiro
Paris, Roseraie de l'Hay-les-Roses, Parc de Bagatelle
Provins, Château de Provins
Usse, Château d'Usse

GREAT BRITAIN
Berkshire, *Windsor,* Saville Gardens
Buckinghamshire, *Clivenden*
Cambridgeshire, *Cambridge,* Cambridge University Botanic Garden
Cheshire, *Chester,* C. and K. Jones Nursery; Knutsford, Fryer's Nursery
Cornwall, *Bodmin,* Lanhydrock House
Derbyshire, *Bakewell,* Chatsworth House Rose Garden, Haddon Hall; *Chesterfield,* Hardwick Hall
Devon, *Torrington,* Rosemoor Garden; *Drewsteignton,* Castle Drogo
Gloucestershire, *Chipping Camden,* Hidcote Manor, Kifstgate Court
Hampshire, *Romsey,* Mottisfont Abbey; *Winchester,* Hillier's Arboretum
Hertfordshire, *Hitchen,* Harkness Rose Garden; *St. Albans,* Bone Mill (The Royal National Rose Society Garden)
Kent, *Maidstone,* Sissinghurst Castle
London, The Queen Mary Rose Gardens, Regent's Park, Kew Gardens, Hampton Court
Norfolk, *Attleborough,* Peter Beales Roses Nursery and Display Garden; *Norwich,* Le Grice Roses Nursery and Display; *Saxthorpe,* Mannington Hall
Nottinghamshire, *Nottingham,* Gregory Roses Nursery, Rosemary Roses Nursery
Oxfordshire, *Oxford,* Oxford University Botanic Gardens
Scotland, *Aberdeen,* Cocker's Roses Nursery and Display Gardens; *Balerno* (Edinburgh), Malleny House; *East Lothian,* Belhaven House, Tyninghame Rose Garden; *Glasgow,* Pollock Park; *Isle of Arran,* Brodick Castle Gardens
Staffordshire, *Albrighton,* David Austin Roses Nursery and Display Gardens; *Rugeley,* Wolesley Rose Gardens, Blithfield Hall
Suffolk, *Claydon* (Ipswich), Lime Kiln Rose Gardens

Surrey, *Woking,* Wisley Garden (The Royal Horticultural Society Gardens)
Wales, *Cardiff,* Roath Park Gardens; *Gwynedd,* Bodnant Gardens
West Sussex, *Handcross,* Nymans
Yorkshire, *Harrogate,* Harlow Carr Gardens; *York,* Castle Howard Gardens

HOLLAND
Amsterdam, Amstelpark Rosarium
The Hague, Westbroekpark Rosarium

INDIA
New Delhi, The Rose Society of India Garden
Punjab, *Chandigarh,* The Zakir Rose Gardens

IRELAND
Adare, Dunraven Arms Hotel
Dublin, St. Ann's
Offaly, Birr Castle

ISRAEL
Jerusalem, Wohl Rose Park

ITALY
Bisuschio (Varese), Villa Cicogna Mozzoni
Cambriglia d'Arezzo, Giardino Fineschi
La Mortola (Ventimiglia), Giardino Hanbury
Monte di Rovagnate (Como), Villa Porlezza
Monza, Villa Reale, Roseto
Pallanza, Giardino Botanico di Villa Taranto
Rome, Giardino Municipale della Rosa
San Bernardino Trana (Turin), Rea Hortus Tranensis
Stresa, Villa Pallavicino
Trieste, Miramare
Valeggio sul Mincio (Verona), Villa Sigurta'

JAPAN
Tokyo, Yatsu-Yuen Rose Gardens

MONACO
Monaco, Roseto di Fontvielle

NEW ZEALAND
Auckland, Bell's Roses Nursery, McGredy Roses International, The Nancy Steen Gardens, The Parnell Rose Gardens
Christchurch, Mona Vale Rose Gardens
Hastings, Frimley Rose Gardens
Napier, The Kennedy Park Rose Gardens
Palmerston North, The Rose Trial Gardens

Timaru, Trevor Griffiths Roses Display Gardens
Wellington, The Lady Norwood Rose Gardens

NORTHERN IRELAND
Belfast, Botanic Gardens, Lady Dixon Park
Newtownards, Dickson Roses Nursery
Saintfield, Rowallane Garden

SOUTH AFRICA
Western Cape Province, Auvellendam, The Drostdy Museum

SPAIN
Granada, Alhambra
Madrid, Rosaleda del Parque del Oeste
Valencia, Jardines del Real

SWEDEN
Goteborg, Rose Garden

SWITZERLAND
Geneva, Parc de la Grange
Sciaffusa, Neuhausen am Rheinfalls Garten

UNITED STATES OF AMERICA
Arizona, *Tucson*, Randolph Park
California, *La Canada*, Descanso Gardens; *Los Angeles*, The Exposition Park Rose Gardens; *San Marino*, The Huntington Botanical Gardens; *San Jose*, Municipal Rose Garden; *Oakland*, Morcom Amphitheater of Roses; *Sacramento*, Capitol Park Rose Garden; *Somis*, Armstrong's Roses Nurseries; *Visalia*, Moore's Miniature Roses Nursery; *Watsonville*, Roses of Yesterday and Today Nursery; *Whittier*, Pageant of Roses Garden
Connecticut, *Hartford*, The Elisabeth Park Rose Garden; *Norwich*, Memorial Rose Garden
Florida, *Cypress Gardens*, All-America Rose Selections Gardens
Georgia, *Thomasville*, Rose Test Garden

Illinois, *Springfield*, Washington Park Rose Garden
Indiana, *Fort Wayne*, The Lakeside Rose Garden
Iowa, *Davenport*, Van der Veer Park; *Des Moines*, Greenwood Park Rose Garden
Kansas, *Topeka*, The Rose and Trial Garden
Louisiana, *Shreveport*, The American Rose Center (American Rose Society Garden)
Massachusetts, *Boston*, The Municipal Rose Gardens; *Jamaica Plain*, Arnold Arboretum
Minnesota, *Minneapolis*, Lake Harriet Rose Gardens
Missouri, *Cape Girardeau*, Capaha Park Rose Display Garden; *Kansas City*, The Municipal Rose Gardens; *St. Louis*, Missouri Botanical Gardens
Montana, *Missoula*, Memorial Rose Garden
New Jersey, *East Millstone*, The Rudolph van der Groot Rose Gardens, Colonial Park Arboretum
New York, *Flushing*, Queens Botanical Gardens; *New York*, Brooklyn Botanic Gardens; *Rochester*, Maplewood Park Rose Garden
North Carolina, *Asheville*, Biltmore House and Gardens
Ohio, *Columbus*, The Park of Roses; *Wooster*, Michael H. Hovath Garden of Legend
Oklahoma, *Tulsa*, The Municipal Rose Garden
Oregon, *Medford*, Jackson & Perkins Nursery Garden; *Portland*, The International Rose Test Garden
Pennsylvania, *Hershey*, The Rose Gardens; *Longwood*, Kennett Square Gardens; *Philadelphia*, Morris Arboretum; Marion W. Revinus Rose Garden; *West Grove*, Robert Pyle Memorial Rose Garden
South Carolina, *Hodges*, Wayside Gardens Nursery; *Orangeburg*, Edisto Gardens
Texas, *Dallas*, Samuell-Grand Municipal Garden; *Fort Worth*, Botanic Garden; *Houston*, Municipal Rose Garden; *Tyler*, Municipal Rose Garden
Washington, *Seattle*, Woodland Park Rose Garden; *Spokane*, The Manito Gardens
Wisconsin, *Hales Corner*, The Boerner Botanical Gardens

Bibliography

Austin, David. *The Rose.* The Antique Collectors' Club, 1987.

Beales, Peter. *Classic Roses.* Collins Harvill, 1985.

———. *Twentieth-Century Roses.* Collins, Harvill, 1988.

Coggiatti, Stelvio. *Il linguaggio delle rose.* Mondadori, 1986.

———. *Les Roses.* Solar, Paris, 1987.

———. *Rose di ieri e di oggi.* Mondadori, 1986.

Dobson, B. R. *Roses on Commerce and Cultivation.* Annual publication, Beverly & Dobson, New York.

Gault, S. M., and Synge, P. M. *The Dictionary of Roses in Color.* Michael Joseph and Ebury Press, 1971 (and following).

Gibson, Michael. *The Book of Classic Old Roses.* Idea Books.

———. *The Book of the Roses.* MacDonald General Book, 1980.

———. *Growing Roses.* Croom Helm, London, 1984.

Griffiths, Trevor. *The Best of Modern Roses.* Pacific, Auckland (New Zealand), 1987.

———. *The Book of Old Roses.* Michael Joseph, 1984.

———. *My World of Old Roses.* Whitcoules, Christchurch (New Zealand), 1987.

Harkness, J. L. *The Makers of Heavenly Roses.* Souvenir Press, 1985.

———. *Roses.* J. M. Dent & Sons, 1978.

———. *The World's Favourite Roses.* McGraw Hill Book Company, 1979.

Jekyll, Gertrude, and Mawley, E. *Roses for English Gardens. Country Life,* 1902 (and various later editions).

Kordes, Wilhelm. *Das Rosenbuck.* Schaper, 1962.

———. *Roses.* Studio Vesta, 1964.

Le Grice, E. *Rose Growing Complete.* Faber & Faber, 1976.

McFarland, J. H. *Modern Roses.* The McFarland Company, 1980.

Modern Roses. *The American Rose Society* (annual since 1917).

Nottle, T. *Growing Old Fashioned Roses in Australia and New Zealand.* Kangaroo Press, 1983.

Paterson, Allen. *The History of the Rose.* Hearn, Stephenson Publishing, 1983.

Philips, R., and Rix, M. *Roses.* Pan Books Ltd.

Roses Annual. The Royal National Rose Society of London (annual since 1917).

Ross, D. *Shrub Roses in Australia.* Deane Ross, 1981.

Sala, Orietta. *Le Mie Rose.* Idealibri, 1988.

Steen, Nancy. *The Charm of Old Roses.* Herbert Jenkins, 1966.

Thomas, Graham Stuart. *Climbing Roses Old and New.* J. M. Dent & Sons, 1979.

———. *Old Shrub Roses.* J. M. Dent & Sons, 1978.

———. *Shrub Roses of Today.* J. M. Dent & Sons, 1974.

Warner, Chris. *Climbing Roses.* Century Hutchinson Ltd., 1987.

Willmott, E. A. *The Genus Rose.* 1914.

Index

314

The illustrations of Aquarius, Bonica, Brandy, Class Act, Mikado, New Year, Oregold, Touch of Class, and Tournament of Roses are reproduced here with the kind permission of All-America Rose Selections, Inc.; Betty Prior, Simplicity, and Gold Medal, with permission of Jackson & Perkins.